Thomas Berry,
Dreamer of the Earth

Thomas Berry, Dreamer of the Earth

The Spiritual Ecology of the Father of Environmentalism

Edited by
Ervin Laszlo and **Allan Combs**

Inner Traditions
Rochester, Vermont • Toronto, Canada

Inner Traditions
One Park Street
Rochester, Vermont 05767
www.InnerTraditions.com

Text paper is SFI certified

Library of Congress Cataloging-in-Publication Data

Thomas Berry, dreamer of the earth : the spiritual ecology of the father of
environmentalism / edited by Ervin Laszlo and Allan Combs.
    p. cm.
  Includes bibliographical references and index.
    ISBN 978-1-59477-395-2
  1. Human ecology—Religious aspects. 2. Human ecology—Philosophy.
3. Philosophy of nature. 4. Berry, Thomas, 1914–2009—Criticism and
interpretation. I. Laszlo, Ervin, 1932– II. Combs, Allan, 1942–
  GF80.T495 2011
  304.2092—dc22

                                                              2010042120

Printed and bound in the United States by Lake Book Manufacturing
The text paper is SFI certified. The Sustainable Forestry Initiative® program
promotes sustainable forest management.

10   9   8   7   6   5   4   3   2   1

Text design and layout by Virginia Scott Bowman
This book was typeset in Garamond Premier Pro with Berkeley Oldstyle and Gill
Sans as display typefaces

Contents

The WorldShift 2012 Declaration

A Declaration of Global Emergency and Emergence

By Ervin Laszlo and David Woolfson

THE CRISIS AND THE OPPORTUNITY

There is no doubt that we are now in a state of global emergency. This unprecedented worldwide crisis is a symptom of a much deeper problem: the current state of our consciousness; how we think about ourselves and our world. We have the urgent need, and now the opportunity, for a complete rethink: to reconsider our values and priorities, to understand our interconnectedness and to shift to a new direction, living in harmony with nature and each other.

Every person, community, and society in the world is already, or will soon be, affected by the global crisis, through climate change, economic breakdown, ecosystem breakdown, population pressure, food and water shortages, resource depletion, and nuclear and other threats. If we continue on our present unsustainable path, by mid-century the Earth could become largely uninhabitable for humans and countless other forms of life. However, total-system collapse could occur much sooner, caused by ecocatastrophes or escalating wars triggered by religious, geopolitical, or resource conflicts.

These threats are real. The underlying causes of the present worldwide crisis have been building momentum for decades and could soon become irreversible. Estimates of when the point of no return will be reached have been reduced from the end of the century, to midcentury, to the next twenty years, and recently to the next five to ten years.

The window of opportunity for shifting our current path and breaking through to a peaceful and sustainable world may be no more than a few years from now. This timeline coincides with the many forecasts and prophecies that speak of the ending of the current cycle of human life on this planet, and the possible dawning of a new consciousness, by the end of the year 2012.

Today, forward-thinking groups and individuals all over the world are addressing the many opportunities presented at this critical time. Designs for sustainable systems, structures, and technologies are being developed and implemented in all sectors, at all levels, and in every society. This global awakening is a hopeful sign of the vitality of the human spirit and our ability to respond to the dangers we now face with insight and creativity.

The totality of our current efforts does not yet match the scope, scale, and urgency of the necessary transformation. But if we collaborate and act with vision, foresight, and commitment we can lay the foundations of a global community that is peaceful, just, and sustainable. We may then ensure our survival and well-being, as well as that of future generations. While the window of time is still open, our top priority as global citizens is to accelerate our evolutionary shift to a planetary consciousness and, together, cocreate this new world and a positive future for humanity.

AN URGENT CALL

We accordingly issue this urgent call to all the peoples of the world to deepen our awareness of both the dangers and the opportunities of the present global crisis. We declare our firm commitment to work together to bring about a timely and positive WorldShift for the survival and well-being of the entire human community and the flourishing of all life on Earth.

www.worldshift2012.org

The Dreamer of the Earth

—

Ervin Laszlo

The last time I saw Thomas Berry was in Mexico in the late 1990s. He remarked that he saw himself as a man of the twentieth century, born in the second decade of that century, and hoping to live to the end of its last decade. In fact, Thomas lived almost a full decade into the twenty-first century.

Berry's thought exceeded his own estimation of himself. He was truly a man not just of the twentieth but also of the twenty-first century: the relevance and meaning of his ideas, his warnings, and his vision became more manifest in the new century than they did in the old. Few thinkers have been as far ahead of their time as Thomas Berry. Many of Berry's writings seem as if they were committed to paper today by a prophetic mind of the twenty-first century.

Berry diagnosed problems that are only now emerging into public awareness. He had amazing foresight. "[T]hrough human presence the forests of the earth are destroyed. Fertile soils become toxic and then wash away in the rain or blow away in the wind. Mountains of human-derived waste grow ever higher. Wetlands are filled in. Each year approximately ten thousand species disappear forever. Even the ozone layer above the earth is depleted."*

---

*All Berry quotations in this chapter are from chapter 5, "The Ecological Age," and chapter 15, "The Dream of the Earth: Our Way to the Future," in Thomas Berry, *The Dream of the Earth,* Sierra Club, 1988.

The human-caused disasters of our time are not limited to the ecology. Berry continued: "Such disturbances in the natural world coexist with all those ethnic, political, and religious tensions that pervade the human realm. Endemic poverty is pervasive in the Third World, while in the industrial world people drown in their own consumption patterns. Population increase threatens all efforts at improvement."

To cope with these problems we need more than better strategies and improved technologies. Berry warned us that we must not mistake the order of magnitude of the challenge. What is needed is "not simply adaptation to a reduced supply of fuels or to some modification in our system of social or economic controls." Yet this is precisely what today, in the final year of Berry's long life, we are attempting to do. Our efforts are centered on finding cheaper sources of energy and on restabilizing our crisis-bound and now obsolete economic-financial system by pumping fresh money into it. We should listen to Berry. "What is happening is something of a far greater magnitude. It is a radical change in our mode of consciousness. Our challenge is to create a new language, even a new sense of what it is to be human."

Berry identified our problems and told us that their order of magnitude includes a change in human consciousness. He told us how our problems have come about: "[W]e are just emerging from a technological entrancement. During this period the human mind has been placed within the narrowest confines it has experienced since consciousness emerged from its Paleolithic phase."

Contrary to the widespread belief that the modern world is immeasurably superior to the world of bygone ages, Berry noted, "Even the most primitive tribes have a larger vision of the universe, of our place and functioning within it, a vision that extends to celestial regions of space and to interior depths of the human in a manner far exceeding the parameters of our own world of technological confinement."

"While former civilizations established our exalted place within the seasonal sequence of the earth's natural rhythms and established those spiritual centers where the meeting of the divine, the natural, and the human could take place, the new effort, beginning in the sixteenth-

and seventeenth-century work of Francis Bacon, Galileo Galilei, and Isaac Newton, was less concerned with such psychic energies than with physical forces at work in the universe and the manner in which we could avail ourselves of these energies to serve our own well-being." The responsibility for this "new effort," to be sure, we should not ascribe to the great pioneers of modern science—for they were themselves deeply spiritual people with vast horizons—but to their followers: the Galileans and the Newtonians who had mistaken a frame of explanation for the mechanistic regularities observed in the natural world for the fundamental nature of that world. It was they who had given birth to what Berry called the "objective world": "a world clearly distinct from ourselves and available not as a means of divine communion, but as a vast realm of natural resources for exploitation and consumption."

Clearly we are facing critical problems, but what is it that needs to be done? Berry's advice remains clear and timely. Basically, he told us, "What we need, what we are ultimately groping toward, is the sensitivity required to understand and respond to the psychic energies deep in the very structure of reality itself." "I suggest," Berry added, "that this is the ultimate lesson in physics, biology, and all the sciences, as it is the ultimate wisdom of tribal peoples and the fundamental teaching of the great civilizations."

But how are we to evolve this sensitivity? Here we should heed Berry again. "We need only to listen to what we are being told through the very structure and functioning of our being." Because, he told us, "the universe is so immediate to us, is such an intimate presence, that it escapes our notice, yet whatever authenticity exists in our cultural creations is derived from these spontaneities within us, spontaneities that come from an abyss of energy and a capacity for intelligible order of which we have only the faintest glimmer in our conscious awareness."

Accessing the spontaneities of the universe calls for a vision that is dreamlike. Imagination functions most freely in dream vision, and so we tend to associate creativity with dream experience. "The dream comes about precisely through the uninhibited spontaneities of which we are speaking," said Berry. "In the beginning was the dream. Through the dream all things were made, and without the dream nothing was made that has been made." Berry also said, "We are immersed in the depths of our own being and of the cosmic order itself in the dream-world that unfolds within us in sleep, or in the visionary moments that seize upon us in our waking hours."

The one aspect of Berry's thinking that calls for updating is his insistence that we reach the spontaneities of the cosmic order by returning to the information that is encoded in our genes. Today we would no longer say that "our bonding with the larger dimensions of the universe comes about primarily through our genetic coding." Genetic coding, to be sure, is the basis, but it is only the template for the more specific guidance that comes about as our genetically coded cells and organs interact with each other, with the surroundings, and with the rest of the universe, and create us, a unique yet natural being. Genetic coding in itself is not "the determining factor." (However, as Plotkin notes below, Berry's insistence on genes and genetic information has a metaphorical element and is not to be taken in a strictly biological sense.) It is through a complex, continuous, and subtle interaction that we maintain "our intimate presence to the functioning of the earth community and to the emergent processes of the universe itself."

But Berry's basic insight remains entirely valid. "[T]he present situation is so extreme that we need to get beyond our existing cultural formation, back to the primary tendencies of our nature itself, expressed in the spontaneities of our being."

We can derive solace and draw courage from Berry's assurances. "[W]e are not left simply to our own rational contrivances. We are supported by the ultimate powers of the universe as they make themselves present to us through the spontaneities within our own beings."

The brightest glimmer of hope shimmering at the darkening horizons of the current global crisis is, in Berry's words, that "the universe is revealing itself to us in a special manner just now. Also the planet Earth and the life communities of the earth are speaking to us through the deepest elements of our nature."

In this brief overview of the unique contemporary relevance of Thomas Berry's thinking, I have left it to Berry to speak to us. Nobody could have articulated the nature of our problems, the reasons for our problems, and the way we should seek to resolve our problems, better than he did.

Thomas Berry, Earth Scholar

A Brief Biography

(1914–2009)

 Born William Nathan Berry in Greensboro, North Carolina, in 1914, Thomas Berry was the third of thirteen children. By age eight he had concluded that commercial values were threatening life on the planet. Three years later he had an epiphany in a meadow, which became a primary reference point for the rest of his life. He later elaborated this experience into what he called "Twelve Principles for Understanding the Universe and the Role of the Human in the Universe Process." The first of these principles states:

> The universe, the solar system, and planet Earth in themselves and in their evolutionary emergence constitute for the human community the primary revelation of that ultimate mystery whence all things emerge into being.

At age twenty Berry entered a monastery of the Passionist order (he was ordained in 1942), and, traveling widely, he began examining the cultural history and foundations of diverse cultures and their relations with the natural world.

He received his doctorate in history from the Catholic University of America, with a thesis on Giambattista Vico's philosophy of history. He then studied Chinese language and Chinese culture in China and learned Sanskrit in order to study the traditions of religion in India. Later he assisted in an educational program for the T'boli tribal peoples of South Cotabataon, a Philippine island, and he taught the cultural history of India and China at universities in New Jersey and New York from 1956 to 1965. He was director of the History of Religions graduate program at Fordham University from 1966 to 1979. He founded and then directed, from 1970 to 1995, the Riverdale Center of Religious Research in Riverdale, New York. Berry studied and was influenced by the work of Teilhard de Chardin, and from 1975 to 1987 he was the president of the American Teilhard Association. He also studied Native American culture and shamanism.

WORKS

Thomas Berry's books include:

- *The Historical Theory of Giambattista Vico* (1949)
- *Buddhism* (1968)
- *The Religions of India* (1972)
- *The Dream of the Earth* (1988)
- *Befriending the Earth* (with Thomas Clarke, 1991)
- *The Universe Story from the Primordial Flaring Forth to the Ecozoic Era: A Celebration of the Unfolding of the Cosmos* (with physicist Brian Swimme, 1992)
- *The Great Work: Our Way into the Future* (1999)
- *Evening Thoughts: Reflecting on Earth as Sacred Community* (2006)

Berry also contributed two introductory essays ("Economics: Its Effects on the Life Systems of the World" and "The Earth: A New Context for Religious Unity") to the volume *Thomas Berry and the New Cosmology,* in which Brian Swimme, Caroline Richards, Gregory Baum, and others discuss the implications of Berry's thought for a range of disciplines and paradigms. Berry's "Twelve Principles for Understanding the Universe and the Role of the Human in the Universe Process" offer a postscript to this 1987 work.

In addition to his voluminous output of literary material, he received many honorary doctorate degrees acknowledging his enormous contribution to the environmental field.

1

The University of the Earth

An Introduction to Thomas Berry

——

Allan Combs

I first became aware of Thomas Berry in 1988, soon after he published *The Dream of the Earth*. I was then living in Asheville, North Carolina, a small town snuggled between the Blue Ridge and Smoky Mountains where I taught at a local liberal arts university. The first thing that impressed me about *The Dream of the Earth* was that Thomas had set out something equivalent to an entire university curriculum based on his spiritual vision of the human in relation to the earth and the cosmos.

Traditional liberal arts universities introduce students to broad areas of knowledge in fields such as literature, languages, philosophy, history, mathematics, and science. Back in medieval times an official liberal arts curriculum was divided into methods for understanding and the content to be understood. The methods included logic, rhetoric, and grammar, together known as the *Trivium*. The areas to be understood included geometry, arithmetic, music, and astronomy, or the *Quadrivium*. In contrast, the university in which I taught offered a broad range of liberal arts courses centered around a four-course sequence of cultural and political history courses that began with the earliest Paleolithic societies and led down to the modern world in all its complexities.

In *The Dream of the Earth,* however, Thomas Berry was laying out a different kind of curriculum, one based on an understanding of the cosmos itself and the human place within it. It seemed to me then, and it seems to me now, that nothing could be timelier or more appropriate for the confused age in which we live. I believe it is worth reviewing this curriculum briefly because in it we find a kind of outline of Thomas's most urgent concerns for understanding the realities of our present historical moment and the pressing issues of our future.

Indeed, Thomas launches this project in a chapter titled *The American College in the Ecological Age,* where he sketches out a series for four courses as the backbone of the new curriculum. In order, these start with a first course that is about the birth and evolution of the cosmos as a whole, the beginnings of life, and the transformation of the earth as life evolved and interacted with the nonliving systems that support it. Here the student would begin to understand the place of the human in the larger picture and—within the living systems of the earth itself—the importance of human action on the complex ecologies of Mother Earth and our place as an integral part of this evolving panorama.

The second course would help the student to understand his or her place in the broad picture of human culture and civilization. From this it would also address the call to meaningful action in today's age of challenges. It would follow the growth of human culture from its earliest origins through the development of the great religions and sketch out the beginnings of technology along its long course down to today's complex technological civilization.

The third course would explore the great classical cultures in Eurasia, Africa, and the Americas. While these differ widely in geographical location and the expression of art, religion, and values, at the same time they seem to have developed languages, social structures, technologies, and values that express deeply common human characteristics. Here we also find what Berry terms the grand humanistic religious traditions of each great culture. Understanding these allows the student to appreciate the similarities between seemingly diverse cultural groups and to learn to honor them. He points out that these classical cultures came into existence when humankind's experience of the world was predominantly spatial, while today we are given the mandate of transitioning to an understanding of the world in an ongoing evolutionary perspective. Such a course might help students understand and appreciate both the challenge and the positive potentials for this important transition.

The fourth course in this sequence would focus on the modern scientific-technological phase of cultural development, leading to an exploration of how the human is now interacting dynamically with the natural systems of the earth and what principles are involved in seeking a sustainable future. This exploration would lead effortlessly into the fifth course, which would be an examination of the present ecological age with its dense interdependence between the human and human technology on the one hand, and the natural systems of the earth on the other. Questions of how sustainability might best be achieved would be paramount here. If Thomas were writing *The Dream of the Earth* today, more than twenty-nine years on from its original publication, we can be sure that besides addressing concerns over biodiversity and the quality of life for all living beings, he would address the problem of global warming as well.

The sixth and final course of this sequence would explore emergent values for an ecological age. Here Thomas suggests three general realms of value. The first addresses the reality of the individual as a central feature of our experience. Thomas points out that the history of cosmic evolution, as well as geological and biological evolution, all involve stages in which previously undifferentiated wholes become articulated into separate parts that are still aspects of the greater whole. The amorphous plasma that filled space immediately after the primal big bang became differentiated into the first subatomic particles, which in time formed a range of more complex particles, ultimately leading toward innumerable varieties of molecules. The latter was the basis of biological evolution with its increasing diversity continuing right up to the beginning of the present ecological age, when activities of the human on a planetary scale have reversed this trend. Understanding this story, and our place in it, is vital to appreciating our proper place on twenty-first-century Earth and how we might act as positive agents of facilitation rather than as a destructive disease agent.

Thomas's second value is subjectivity. Here he observes that it is through our interior subjectivity that we experience the more profound aspects of ourselves and the world around us. The poet, the thinker, the artist, the scientist all take their inspiration from an interior dimension that also brings us into communion with other human beings as well as the rich life that we first meet in the external world. It is this dimension, in fact, that grows into the third value realm, that of communion itself. Not only are we as human beings in communion with those persons we live with and love, but with all other life as well. In the forms of cooperation and symbiosis this is an essential aspect of evolution and life in general. Perhaps Thomas is most often quoted for his observation that the universe is not merely a collection of objects and organisms but "a communion and a community. We ourselves are that communion become conscious of itself."[1]

Now, having touched on the above core notions in Thomas's thought as they are reflected in the six basic courses he recommends for his university curriculum, let us take a quick walk around the quad of a typical campus and reflect on some of the fields of learning that might be enriched by his influence.

We might first come across the art department. There, along with the traditional course offerings in drawing, painting, photography, sculpture, and silk screening, we would hope to see artists and students exploring the beauty of the natural world, not only through these traditional forms but perhaps also working more closely with nature as seen in Andy Goldsworthy's creations, using objects such as wood, stone, and ice in the wild landscape.

We would also hope that the celebration of the natural world and the human as well as other living beings essential to it would be explored through music and dance. For example, the Greek composer

Vangelis Papathanassiou, perhaps best known for scores to films such as *Chariots of Fire* and *Blade Runner,* considers much of his work to be "Earth Music," reflecting the sounds and rhythms of nature. Likewise there exists a tradition in literature, and especially American literature, that celebrates nature in poetry, essays, and novels. From Henry David Thoreau's *Walden* and Walt Whitman's *Leaves of Grass,* to John Muir's many essays on nature, to Peter Matthiessen's *Snow Leopard* and David Abram's *The Spell of the Sensuous,* we find a great living tradition of the literature of wild nature. A cultural history of the human's relation to nature in poetry and art is also found in Robert Bly's *News of the Universe.*

We might also hope to find the Department of Economics as well as the Business School exploring the emerging field of Green Economics, with its stress on quality rather than quantity, on the importance of sustainability and regeneration, on the value of individuals and communities of all kinds, and on ecosystems, rather than on the accumulation of money or material wealth. Indeed, with prophetic insight, in *The Dream of the Earth* Thomas introduces the notion of an *earth deficit* that overarches such purely financial indices as the GNP.

> Seldom does anyone speak of the deficit involved in the closing down of the basic life system of the planet through abuse of the air, the soil, the water, and the vegetation. As we have indicated, the *earth deficit* is the real deficit, the ultimate deficit, the deficit in some of its major consequences so absolute as to be beyond adjustment from any source in heaven or on earth. Since the earth system is the ultimate guarantee of all deficits, a failure here is a failure of the last resort. Neither economic viability nor improvement in life conditions for the poor can be realized in such circumstances. These can only worsen, especially when we consider the rising population levels throughout the developing world.[2]

Fortunately, much of the world is beginning to wake up to these problems today, but it is the eleventh hour and much is to be done.

It is especially important for universities to teach this message of this urgency to young people, but not in terms of pessimistic scenarios of lost resources and lost hope, but rather in terms of optimistic challenges that can be met by their own generation.

We would hope that the School of Law would value the importance of the environment and the quality of life of all beings that live on our planet. The historical Enlightenment was a dramatic step forward toward modern civilization, creating in the United States the first great liberal democracy of the world, one that still lasts today. But the stress on the individual and personal rights, when combined with the "American Dream," the idea that everyone can achieve unlimited wealth and success for themselves, has led to a disastrous growth of greed along with a widespread unwillingness to work toward common cooperative goals.

Moving along around the quad, the department of psychology might offer courses that address the inner depth dimension of human experience. No one has written more eloquently and profoundly on this topic than William James, in his *Principles of Psychology* and *The Varieties of Religious Experience,* both classics as relevant today as when they were written more than a hundred years ago. Students might also investigate the mythic and archetypal dimensions of the human soul. In this regard, Thomas notes of the great works of art and literature that "all of these derive from the visionary power that is experienced most profoundly when we are immersed in the depths of our own being and of the cosmic order itself in the dreamworld that unfolds within us in our sleep, or in those visionary moments that seize upon us in our waking hours. There we discover the Platonic forms, the dreams of Brahman, the Hermetic mysteries, the divine ideas of Thomas Aquinas, the infinite worlds of Giordano Bruno, the world soul of the Cambridge Platonists, the self-organizing universe of Ilya Prigogine, the archetypal world of C. G. Jung."[3]

Needless to say, for the university inspired by Thomas Berry's vision, psychology and religion would have considerable overlap. In-depth studies of the words of great spiritual teachers such as Meister Eckhart, Lao-tzu, Ramana Maharshi, Shankara, and Nagarjuna would be among the offerings, as well as deep explorations of the great religious traditions themselves. The latter would overlap with courses offered by the department of history, which in turn would grow out of the third core course described above.

The physical and natural sciences, especially astronomy and biology, might offer courses that examine the deep story of the unfolding of the cosmos and life within it, again filling out the vision developed in the core courses. Many of the books by Thomas Berry himself, as well as Brian Swimme, Lewis Thomas, Lynn Margulis, and others—including more advanced technical texts—might be read to flesh out this story, to understand the vital roles played by cooperation, symbiosis, and in Thomas's word, communion.

The department of philosophy is ideally where it all comes together. Indeed, it has been said that philosophy is the heart of a great university, and a good case could be made for Thomas Berry being a philosopher himself. His grand vision of an evolving cosmos, with life as an integral part of the overall picture if not the centerpiece of it, has a long tradition in Western thought, starting with Georg Wilhelm Friedrich Hegel, whose philosophy of a universe in which the Divine expresses itself though living beings, and particularly through the history of the human being and human consciousness, created a dominant theme in European philosophy that lasted for much of the nineteenth century. Then, by the turn of the twentieth century the widely read French philosopher Henri Bergson had become a major figure in evolutionary thinking about consciousness. Not unlike Hegel, but in a more widely accessible style, he considered the advance of consciousness itself to be the centerpiece of evolution. His book, *Creative Evolution,* is still important reading for the student of evolution, consciousness, and spirituality.

Bergson's thinking was deeply influential on the Jesuit philosopher, cosmologist, and paleontologist Pierre Teilhard de Chardin, who would be the most important intellectual and spiritual forerunner of Thomas Berry. Teilhard de Chardin's works, such as *The Phenomenon of Man* in 1955, brought mid-twentieth-century scientific thinking into direct dialogue with spiritual, metaphysical, and evolutionary thought. This occurred in such a way so as to inspire a whole generation of spiritual and intellectual seekers looking for answers to deep questions about the human's place in the universe without abandoning serious science or intellectual integrity.

In some ways Thomas Berry might be viewed as Teilhard de Chardin freed of the chains of the heavily reductionist science of the midcentury and the still oppressive policies of the church. It is as if all the great vision and wildness compressed in Teilhard de Chardin's intellectual legacy is released in Thomas's free, shamanic, and unleashed vision of the living and evolving cosmos.

Now we have completed a short stroll about the quad and had a brief acquaintance with many of the important ideas in Thomas's thought. As co-editor of this collection of wonderful essays about Thomas and his legacy, each written by one of the leading evolutionary visionaries of our time, I welcome you to these pages.

2

The Emerging Ecozoic Period

Thomas Berry

In biological terms, planet Earth is at the end of the Cenozoic period. This period is being terminated by the industrial economy that humans have imposed on the planet during these past two centuries. In this context the major life-giving systems of the planet, the air, the water and the soil, are severely diminished in their life-giving capacities.

To establish a viable situation for the earth community requires a transition from the Cenozoic to what might be termed the Ecozoic period of earth history. (The *Ecozoic* is a newly invented term; a possible designation for the newly emerging period.) The Cenozoic is that period of the evolution of the living systems of the earth that have developed over these past 65 million years and which are being extinguished by our present industrial economy. The Ecozoic is the emerging period of the integral life community, the fourth in the sequence of life periods that are generally designed as the Paleozoic (600–220 million years ago), the Mesozoic (220–65 million years ago), and the Cenozoic (65 million years ago until the present).

Before giving a full description of the Ecozoic period and the

This chapter was previously published in *Cooperation: Beyond the Age of Competition*, edited by Allan Combs (New York & London: Gordon & Breach, 1992).

historical role that it is called upon to fulfill, we must first appreciate the Cenozoic period in the full grandeur of its creativity, in its role in bringing the human species into being and providing the context for the unfolding of human life until the present.

The Cenozoic could be considered the lyric period of the evolutionary process, the period of the flowers, the birds, the mammals. For sixty-five million years, wave upon wave of life appeared. Then came the human. Hominid types appeared roughly three million years ago, types that died out long ago. The appearance of humans from which we can trace our own descent occurs as far back as roughly two hundred thousand years. This early human period, culturally identified as the Paleolithic, or Old Stone Age, lasted from until some twelve thousand years ago when the Neolithic, or New Stone Age, appears in this unfolding process.

Until recently we have considered this Neolithic period of permanent village settlements and the domestication of plants and animals as, unquestionably, an admirable achievement on the part of the human, the moment when we began to be human in some full sense of the word. We did not see the dangers inherent in this domestication process. This was a movement of humans to take control of the spontaneous processes whereby the various life systems of Earth were mutually supportive and underwent their seasonal renewal each year. The danger was that humans would seek to impose their mechanistic processes on the biological functioning of the natural life systems, mechanistic processes that would eventually, in the twentieth century, be extended until these controls were felt throughout the entire planet. True wilderness, true independence from the human, would be severely diminished, if not obliterated.

Even more than a reassessment of developments in the Neolithic period, we need to reassess the civilizations that came after this period that have dominated the planetary process over these past five thousand years. These civilizations provided the context for that vast expansion of the human realm. The great cities were built, human learning was expanded, the arts developed, roads were built, and commerce expanded. The great religious centers evolved, the temples built, the ceremonies made ever more gorgeous in their expression. All this went with a pervasive human arrogance in relation to the other members of the earth community.

We need especially to rethink the sequence of events that have taken place in the Western world during the past few centuries, the period that we have designated as the period par excellence of "progress." During this period, which has been dominated by the ideal of "progress," we developed our scientific understanding of how the earth functioned and how it could be controlled. We withdrew from our intimate relations with the natural world and increased our controls over the rhythmic functioning of the planet. Enchantment with ourselves and our supposed betterment of the human situation did not permit a critical appraisal of just what we were doing in the larger pattern of earthly affairs.

The Neolithic period, the Civilization period, and our modern period of progress have so far been judged not by their effects on the integral functioning of the planet, but by advance in our human controls over the earth, by our rational understanding, the abundance of our food supply, our control over illness, our consumer satisfaction, our capacity to travel more rapidly from one place to another, and by our capacity for communication. We judged progress by its benefits for ourselves.

We were insensitive to the effects this was having on the natural world. We built our dams for electrical power and thus profoundly disturbed the flow of the rivers. We forced the soil to produce, not according to its own rhythm, but according to the demands we made through our chemical fertilizers. We took the petroleum from the earth and used it for heat, energy, fertilizers, plastics, fibers, and a multitude of other uses, little realizing that we were disturbing the wonderful balance of the elements that nature had worked out over the millennia. We paid little attention to the effects that would result from the carbon and sulfur compounds that we were pouring into the atmosphere.

Suddenly in these late decades of the twentieth century, we are becoming aware of our profound disruption of the natural world, the extinction of species, the killing of the rain forests, the pollution of the airsphere and the watersphere as well as the landsphere. All of this is now coming under judgment.

The supposed higher development of our human mode of being through our humanist arrogance and our religious fixations is being reexamined. Their effects on the planet, its life systems, and even on ourselves must now be reevaluated in terms of what is happening to the planet on which we live and on which we depend absolutely for survival.

We have indeed gained in our empirical knowledge of the universe in terms of its physical functioning. We know the physical structure and functioning of the universe and of the planet Earth as no other age has known the natural world about us.

THE EMERGING ECOZOIC PERIOD

But in the process we have become autistic. We have lost our capacity for communication with the natural world in its inner life, its spirit mode. We find ourselves illiterate as regards the languages of the natural world. We do not hear the voices of the trees, the rivers, the birds, the mountains, the animals, or the insects. We have become a death-dealing presence.

We now have a new task before us. We must completely revise our understanding of the earth story, the life story, the human story, and the Western story; for indeed our new situation reveals the true reality of what we have been doing. It reveals the dark powers of both the humanist and the religious traditions of our Western world, powers that have now been communicated throughout the entire human community. Even beyond this, it reveals the dangers to itself that the earth brought forth in producing the human species.

This danger was in the termination of the magnificent florescence of the Cenozoic period. That danger has become a reality in this late twentieth century. The Cenozoic is definitely terminated. The life systems that were so significant in this period are now so severely damaged that they are no longer capable of continuing their successive waves of creativity. They are all in a state of regression. Our biophysical planet is under assault in its every aspect.

Yet neither Earth history nor human history is concluded. There is a future that is taking shape. A movement toward the healing of the earth can be observed even amid the many devastating processes that are still functioning. As we rewrite the story of the past and consider the realities of the present, we have already begun the shaping of the future.

As we proceed with this immense task we need to recognize both our limitations and our possibilities. We cannot make a blade of grass, but there may not in the future be a blade of grass unless it is willed by us, fostered and protected by us. There is a vast disproportion between our destructive and our constructive capacities. Although we can do almost nothing creative in the biological order ourselves, we can severely damage the entire biosphere of the planet. We can eliminate an immense number of species, but we cannot create anew any enduring species. The millions of species in the Cenozoic period were brought into being independently of any human influence.

A primary aspect of the Ecozoic period is that we recognize the larger community of life as our primary referent in terms of reality and value. This locating of the higher reality and the higher value in the larger community is absolutely primary. All species must be granted their habitat, their freedom, and their range of life expression. The more complex life systems are proportionately more rather than less dependent on the simpler life systems. The simpler forms can generally survive the elimination of the more complex forms, but the more complex forms cannot survive without the simpler forms. If the plankton in the sea cease their functioning, the multitude of living beings on the planet will cease to exist for lack of oxygen. So with the bacteria in the soil. If the bacteria cease to function, then the soil will not be able to produce the foods needed by the various forms of life. So with the worms and the insects. These perform immensely important roles in the single web of life; they deserve full recognition for the role that they fulfill.

All the human professions must recognize their prototype and their primary resource in the integral functioning of the earth community. The natural world itself is the primary economic reality, the primary educator, the primary governance, the primary healer, the primary presence of the sacred, the primary moral value. In economics it is clear that our human economy is derivative from the earth economy. To glory in a rising Gross National Product with an irreversibly declining Gross Earth Product is an economic absurdity. The only viable human economy is one that is integral with the earth economy.

Education is already late in its revision but we can expect that it will, in the future, be extensively altered. Education will be defined as knowing the story of the universe, of the planet Earth, of life and consciousness, all as a single story. In our governance we are moving from a limited democracy to a more comprehensive biocracy. Already we can envisage a constitution not simply for humans on this continent, but for the entire North American community. A beginning has been made in the legislation requiring environmental impact statements before any major project affecting the environment can be undertaken.

Already the medical profession begins to see that the well-being of the ecosystems of the planet is a prior condition for the well-being of the human. We cannot have well humans on a sick planet, not even with all our medical technologies.

Religion begins to appreciate that the primary sacred community is the earth community itself, that the human community becomes sacred through its participation in the larger planetary community. In mortality we are expanding our moral sensitivity beyond suicide, homicide, and genocide to include biocide and geocide—evils that were not recognized in our civilizational traditions until recently.

The sciences and the humanities, business and religion, the arts and sciences—all these divisions of learning are overcoming their isolation from each other. Even though the distinctive roles of each need always be recognized, they will in the future become much more integral with each other. But all our professions and institutions need to be appreciated in the light of the single story that governs the entire Earth as well as the entire human process.

We begin to rethink the structure and functioning of our cities. No longer will we endure without protest the oppression of the automobile as the primary factor in our city architecture. Already cities are being redesigned to bring streams above ground rather than condemning them to flow through our sewers. Our cities begin to be places for habitation, not merely by humans but also by other life-forms. We begin to make provisions for the birds and the various animals that are proper to the region.

Earlier we were concerned simply with our own limited area. We withdrew from the major forces of life into the realm of our own limited controls. We developed our individual self with a neglect of our community self, our relation with planet Earth, and with the entire natural order that constitutes the larger self of our own being.

As the Ecozoic era comes into its full expression, the healing of the past and the shaping of the future are becoming more effective. The possibilities and the promise of the future become clear. As we finally become familiar with the language and the wisdom of the winds and the sea and the land and all the unnumbered forms of life that form the great community of the earth, we finally realize that we are earthlings, that we are born out of the earth, that we have no future except within the larger Earth community.

3

Some Thoughts on Thomas Berry's Contributions to the Western Spiritual Tradition

———

Matthew Fox

Caribbean poet and Nobel Prize–winner Derek Wallcott says: "For every poet it is always morning in the world; history a forgotten, insomniac night. The fate of poetry is to fall in love with the world in spite of history."

I believe Walcott names an accomplishment of Thomas Berry's poetic and mystical side—Thomas calls all of us to fall in love with the world *in spite of the folly of human history.* It is a major challenge and Thomas creates a context when he says "ecology is functional cosmology"—a context in which we can recover the zeal that comes from falling in love with the world once again. He puts our own personal and collective histories into context, and he puts the context into a sacred context by reminding us that the primary sacrament is the universe itself. Every other sacrament, being, and action is derivative of that holy sacrament.

TEILHARD DE CHARDIN AND THOMAS BERRY

When I think of Thomas, I am reminded of the great mentor/protégé relationships of Western history. I think of Teilhard de Chardin's influence on Thomas Berry in the same light that I think of Plato's influence on Aristotle and Albert the Great's influence on Thomas Aquinas, for example. Thomas had a mentor and all studies show that when young men have mentors they go into deeper paths and new spirals of achievement.

Let us consider some of the influence of Teilhard on Thomas's thought as we remember that Thomas was a founder and president of the Friends of Teilhard Society in New York. Teilhard, we recall, was too radioactive in his philosophical works to be allowed by the church to be published in his lifetime, but rather than allow his life's work to be forgotten altogether, he bequeathed it not to his Jesuit Order but to a lay woman who published it after his death.

One of the basic issues Teilhard dealt with was the dismal dualism that has so haunted Christian thought at least from St. Augustine onward (and that was derived from Platonism). Augustine, recall, declared that "spirit is whatever is not matter." Aquinas and Eckhart both disagreed with this dualism but so does Teilhard in a very big way. He writes: "Matter and Spirit: These were no longer two things but two *states* or two aspects of one and the same cosmic Stuff, according to whether it was looked at or carried further in the direction in which it is becoming itself or in the direction in which it is disintegrating. Matter is the Matrix of Spirit. Spirit is the higher state of Matter."[1]

We find this nondualism and this flow of matter to spirit and spirit to matter taken for granted and running through all of Berry's work. It shows in his sensitivity and passion for beauty and for the "numinosity" that he so often recognizes in the habits of nature, whether microcosmic or macrocosmic. Berry puts poetry and substance into the new direction of a nondualistic consciousness, one that Teilhard struggled to lay out and that Aquinas and Eckhart before him also paid a price for preaching. (Aquinas taught that spirit was the "élan" in everything including matter, that spirit was also our capacity for knowing all things, and that body and soul were "con-substantial.")

Another area where Teilhard and Berry connect is their passion for their work, their passion for announcing and defending the earth. Teilhard writes that "to understand the world knowledge is not enough. You must see it, touch it, live in its presence and drink the vital heat of existence in the very heart of reality."[2] Seeing, touching, living, drinking the vital heat—those are metaphors for his own passionate love of the earth. Anyone who knew Thomas or heard him speak also felt the passion in his work. His was not an abstract or detached attitude of knowledge about something. It was a love affair, a passion; a vital heat rose in the room when he spoke. This was wisdom, not just knowledge. Thomas was a wisdom teacher not a knowledge teacher. Wisdom includes both knowledge and heart, mind and passion. And of course a call to creativity because wisdom is always present in creativity. "A completely new type of creativity is needed," Berry said. "This creativity must have as its primary concern the survival of the earth in its functional integrity." Berry was a warrior on behalf of Mother Earth. He was a Green Man in the fullest sense of that word.

Teilhard does not dwell on the story of entropy in matter but waxes joyful about nature's youthfulness and constant newness. He writes: "Till the very end of time matter will always remain young, exuberant, sparkling, newborn for those who are willing."[3] Here he calls on the attitude of the observer. If you approach nature tired and cynical and pessimistic you may very well project that pessimism onto nature. But "for those who are willing," nature offers ample evidence of a bias in favor of youth, exuberance, sparkle, and newness.

Those of us who knew Thomas Berry or heard him speak or read his works know which choice he made. He was one "of the willing." His spirit, while never naive and always critical, was also profoundly hopeful. He was renewed by his studies of nature. Nature itself gave him a perspective on resiliency. I once heard him respond to a student's question of despair about the Bush presidency, and Thomas responded: "Bush will not be president forever." This was a perspective that no doubt kept his hope alive. Anthropocentrism can be very debilitating. It can suck life out of one's spirit. Attunement to nature's ways often reignites life and renews it. It did that for Teilhard and for Berry.

Thomas, like Teilhard, was very attuned to beauty. The language of beauty permeates his work and his commitment to an aesthetic (not effete) awareness was visible to all who read his books or heard him speak. He had a poetic flare in the very language he spoke or wrote in. This parallels Teilhard's teaching that "purity is not a debilitating separation from all created reality, but an impulse carrying one through all forms of created beauty."[4] From that perspective, Berry sported the kind of *purity* that Teilhard championed—not a purity of distance and separation, but a purity that awakened curiosity and interest and study of "all forms of created beauty." Berry had that sense of love of beauty; his hungry curiosity and undying search for beauty burned in his heart and mind.

Teilhard champions a "cosmic sense" when he says that "the cosmic sense must have been born as soon as humanity found itself facing the frost, the sea and the stars. And since then we find evidence of it in all our experience of the great and unbounded: in art, in poetry, and in religion."[5] Thomas's lifework, we might say, was to rekindle that *cosmic sense* that ought to be in art, poetry, and religion. Yes, and in education too. The modern age cut us off from a cosmic sense when it declared the universe was a machine and when it set man up as the final arbiter of existence. The beauty and aesthetic was drained from the universe and the earth itself by that worldview. No animals or plants housed souls according to Descartes. But Berry, in the tradition of Teilhard but also in the tradition of Aquinas and Saint Paul (of whom a recent scholar has written that he held a "metacosmic" sense of the Christ[6]) insisted that the cosmos itself needs to be accepted as "the primordial sacred community, the macrophase mode of every religious tradition, the context in which the divine reality is revealed to itself in that diversity which in a special manner is 'the perfection of the universe.'"[7] To recover a sense of the sacred, one recovers a sense of the cosmos, of a whole that we all serve.

Thomas is explicit in placing his vision in the lineage of the Cosmic Christ written of in John's Gospel (Christ as the "light in all things") and Paul, and of Aquinas and Teilhard when he writes: "If Saint John and Saint Paul could think of the Christ form of the universe, if Aquinas could say that the whole universe together participates in the divine goodness more perfectly and represents it better than any single creature whatever, and if Teilhard could insist that the human gives to the entire cosmos its most sublime mode of being, then it should not be difficult to accept the universe itself as the primordial sacred community."[8]

Of course our sense of the cosmos has been profoundly deepened by our awareness of evolution both on Earth and in the universe. Teilhard was explicit about the wonder and awe he underwent on studying evolution (what a far cry this is from silly fundamentalists who, because they do not value awe but stick to literalism, miss the sacred dimensions of the evolution story). Teilhard writes: "That magic word 'evolution' which haunted my thoughts like a tune: which was to me like unsatisfied hunger, like a promise held out to me, like a summons to be answered."[9] Evolution became a vocation, a calling, for Teilhard. A magical calling. It was the same for Berry, whose work is not an argument about evolution either for or against, but a journey with evolution and its profound and meaningful gifts to our sense of the whole and our sense of the sacred.

Indeed, Berry goes further. He believes that it will take a "shamanic personality, a type that is emerging once again in our society," to bring about this deeper sense of the sacred. Not philosophers, not priests, not prophets, but shamans are needed. "This intimacy with our genetic endowment and through this endowment with the larger cosmic process, is not primarily the role of the philosopher, priest, prophet or professor. It is the role of the shamanic personality."[10] Berry used to say that the two biggest failures of the twentieth century were education and religion. Here he seems to be naming why they so failed. Lacking a sense of intimacy with the cosmic process, neither priest nor professor is offering what the young need today. The young need something greater than "our own rational contrivances." We need to become "sensitized to the spontaneities" of the "ultimate powers of the universe" and this "intimacy with our genetic endowment" is the work of shamans. Maybe if we had shaman schools (instead of what Berry labeled present education—"barbaric academia") neither education nor religion would be failing us so profoundly.

THE CALL TO SHAMANHOOD

Shamanhood was an important category to Thomas Berry. (He once told me that he considered me more of a shaman than a teacher or priest, and only lately have I begun to explore the message he was transmitting to me by that observation.) In a recent book of interviews and commentaries with the late poet William Everson, author Steven Herrmann talks at length about "The Shaman's Call." In hearing his reflections I hear very much the echoes of Thomas Berry's at-easeness with shamanhood, his call for more shamanhood, and his recognition of the rise of shamanhood in our time. Everson was a beat poet who became a Dorothy Day Catholic and a Dominican brother and later exited the order to "recover his aboriginal roots."[11] He says he "took the figure of the shaman as the most direct route to a 'recovery of nature.'" Berry was always on the lookout for routes to a recovery of nature.

Part of the journey of the shaman as Everson understood it is through animism, "back into the instinctual, which is the basis of the archetypal."[12] Berry too continually calls us back to our instincts; beyond the rational. Writes Berry: "None of our existing cultures can deal with this situation out of its own resources. We must invent, or reinvent, a sustainable human culture by a descent into our pre-rational, our instinctive, resources. Our cultural resources have lost their integrity. They cannot be trusted."[13]

Shamanism was Everson's path back to the *unus mundus,* or what Jung called the "one world" of unitary consciousness. Trance-like techniques are employed by shamans through drumming and dancing and by poet-shamans through writing or speaking a poem aloud. Trance is invoked.

The shaman often carries a wound, but often this wound is that of the larger community itself. "Shamans are, nevertheless, highly susceptible to psychic infections from their communities, because their wounds remain 'open, susceptible to impression from the outside.'" Was not much of Berry's strength shamanistic insofar as he was both carrying and then articulating the profound wound of the community—anthropocentrism, our being cut off from the earth and our deepest animal instincts, from the universe and the community with all beings? This is the work of the shaman who "descends in trance, through wounds in the collective psychic structure, like a diving bird, to awaken images of healing for the race."[14] Berry named the collective psychosis of our race: our split from the rest of nature.

The shaman's wound "is also the source of the poet's greatest creativity, powers, ego-strength, and gift to the community."[15] How much of Berry's strength and perseverance in study and in telling his insight to the world was inspired by his wound, which was also our wound? Jung proposed that "the earth and psyche are not two, separate realities, but one 'unitary world' which he called the *unus mundus*." Surely this is Thomas Berry's passion also—to move us all to a sense of the *unus mundus,* a new (and ancient?) marriage of Earth and psyche that the modern consciousness in particular devastated to the point that, in Berry's words, we are all "autistic" in our relationship to nature. A shaman heals the community. Berry did that. He was more than a priest and more than a professor. Eliade wrote that the shaman "is the great master of ecstasy." Berry did not just write of gloom and doom; he also indulged in memories of ecstasy. He did not preach guilt so much as beauty, harmony, and health. He motivated others through a spirituality of blessing more than guilt.

I believe we might safely argue that Thomas Berry, not unlike Walt Whitman, Ralph Waldo Emerson, and William Everson, was himself a shaman calling us to our collective shamanhood, that is to re-experience the ecstatic trance, the "numinous" relationship with the cosmos, that is our birthright and is also our way back to our own healing, our own instincts, our own *ground*—precisely as Meister Eckhart uses that term to denote the Godhead, the "Source without a source" (Aquinas), the Mystery without a name that will never be given a name.

THOMAS BERRY, MOSES, AND HILDEGARD

Speaking in general terms and using a biblical metaphor, I think Thomas stands up as a kind of new Moses leading all religious people, people of religious sensibilities and certainly Christians, out of a bondage of a land of anthropocentrism to a land of cosmology and ecology, a land flowing with milk and honey, a land that promises to respond to the great needs of the great human heart. He leads us out of the land of "autism" into a land of renewed communication with other beings and other species who are in fact very eager to communicate, to reveal themselves to us. He leads us out of the land of "academic barbarism" (his words—which I love) to a land of educational responsibility where the power of knowledge is subsumed to the greater common good, where Ph.D.s, instead of destroying the earth (his observation), are employing wisdom to save the Earth and her beauty. He leads us out of a land of psychologism where disenchantment, cynicism, trivia, inertia, violence, commercialism, and what Thomas calls the "illusory world of advertising" reign, into a land where enchantment, beauty, wonder, and intimacy become our values—a place where *caring* matters.

He leads us out of the land of domestication to revelry of the sacred, which always has something in common with the wild. For example, he writes: "Wildness we might consider as the root of the authentic spontaneities of any being. It is that wellspring of creativity whence comes the instinctive activities that enable all living beings to obtain their food, to find shelter, to bring forth their young: to sing and dance and fly through the air and swim through the depths of the sea. This is the same inner tendency that evokes the insight of the poet, the skill of the artist and the power of the shaman." How beautifully Thomas marries the wild energy, the sacred energy of the more than human world with human creativity in that powerful passage. It is such a reminder that we are capable as a species of domesticating even Divinity Itself, making Divinity into our tidy images. Thomas leads us out of the land of boredom to a sense of awe, and with awe comes gratitude and with awe comes reverence—what Thomas calls a "sense of the numinous." In this way he is setting faith in the premodern context of the sacredness of all creation, of cosmology, of the more than human.

If a "new Moses" is too strong a term for some to name Thomas's contribution, then surely we could settle on another term—prophet. The primary work of the prophet, as Rabbi Heschel teaches, is to "interfere." And Thomas is nothing if not a great interferer. He is so subtle about it they haven't caught up with him yet. Prophets wake a sleeping people, and Thomas does that. Prophets cry in the wilderness, and Thomas does that. Prophets call people who are wallowing in injustice and neglect back to justice, and Thomas does that. He calls us to Eco-Justice, which is the necessary context for all other justice struggles—be they economic, racial, gender, or class. He calls us as the prophets of old did to the Great Work and thus to leave trivial work behind. He calls us to reach for the Ecozoic Age and indeed, in his thoroughly challenging phrase, to "reinvent our species."

In trying to assess Thomas's contribution to Western spirituality, I believe we are assisted by his own work. In a brief essay on Hildegard of Bingen he wrote this about Western spirituality: "Thus far Christians have been so concerned with redemption out of this world, so attached to their spiritual life development or their social mission of reconciliation that they have had little time for their serious attention to the earth. Nor do Christians seem to be aware of the futility of social transformations proceeding on an historical-industrial rather than on a comprehensive ecological basis. . . . We find relatively few Christian guides in the past to enlighten or to inspire us to a more functional relationship between the human and the natural worlds."[16] But then Thomas offers three examples of the past: Benedict offered an agrarian model, he being the father of course of Western monasticism; Francis of Assisi offered a model based on the universal community of creatures; Hildegard is a third model with her sense of the earth as "a region of delight, we might almost say of pagan delight," which she has found from within her own experience and in a "unique model of Christian communion." Hildegard writes: "The entire world has been embraced by this kiss [of God and creation]." Thomas adds: "Because of this erotic bond, the earth becomes luxuriant in its every aspect."[17] I propose that Thomas enfolds Benedict's agrarian model, Francis's community model, and Hildegard's erotic model into his work.

THOMAS BERRY AND THOMAS AQUINAS

I see in Thomas Berry's work a fourth model, which I would call the cosmic scientific model. I think the precursor of this model is in fact Thomas's own namesake whom he quotes so often, St. Thomas Aquinas of the thirteenth century who was condemned three times by the church before they canonized him a saint. Like Thomas Berry, Aquinas had the imagination, the scientific curiosity, and the courage to propose a whole new direction for Christian theology in his day. The direction was that of incorporating science, and of course the breakthrough scientist of Aquinas's day was Aristotle, a pagan who came to Europe by way of Islam. Aristotle came double-tainted into Christianity, and this is why Aquinas was condemned three times: he was working overtime with those who were more than Christian.

Some of Aquinas's observations follow. "Faith comes in two volumes: Nature and the Bible."[18] We all know Thomas Berry's notorious remark that he has repeated more than once—that we should "put the Bible on a shelf for twenty years." This is simply the logical conclusion that we have been overdoing the book-bit in the name of revelation at least since the invention of the printing press. Why is it that by now *every* seminary, every school that pretends to be training spiritual leaders, does not have scientists on its faculty telling us the revelation of nature, its mysticism, and the ethics to be derived from that as well as biblical theologians? We must find the balance anew between the revelation of nature and the revelation of the Bible.

In fact, in the Bible there is a whole tradition—the wisdom tradition—which scholars now agree was the tradition of the historic

Jesus, which is total nature mysticism. One prevalent teaching of scholars today is that Jesus as a child, being considered illegitimate, was excluded from the synagogue, so he went out and played in nature while others were meeting to pray indoors, and that radicalized him. It comes through in all of his parables and all of his teachings, which are all nature-based. Wisdom literature is not based on reading books. Jesus was illiterate like most of his country people.

Another connection between Aquinas and Berry—Berry is of course carrying this in all new directions—is Aquinas's observation that "every human person is *capax universi* (capable of the universe)." That's who we are as a species. That's how big we are and neither our souls nor our hearts nor our minds will be satisfied and therefore relieved of temptations to greed and power until they are reset in the context of cosmology and the universe itself. In this regard the exciting teachings of the universe story in our time that emerges from the work of Thomas and Brian Swimme in recovering a universe story fulfills Aquinas's observation.

Consider for example the great Otto Rank, the father of humanistic psychology who broke with Freud over many issues. Rank came to the conclusion that the number one problem for human beings is the feeling of separation that begins with leaving the womb, which was our universe for nine months, and the rest of life is about trying to find a reunion with the cosmos. He says: "We surrender ourselves in art or love to a potential restoration with the union of the cosmos which once existed and was then lost." He talks about "original wound" (much better than "original sin") that haunts our species. This is that wound: that we feel separated from the cosmos. He says the only solution is the *Unio Mystica,* being one with the all, in tune with the cosmos. And indigenous people all know about this. Rank said: "This identification is an echo of an original identity not only merely of child and mother but of everything living. Witness the reverence of the primitives for animals. In humans identification aims at reestablishing a lost identity with the cosmic process that has to be surrendered and continuously reestablished in the course of self-development."[19] Thomas Berry's work is a profound work of human healing because it restores that lost identity and relationship and passion between the human and the cosmos.

Gaston Bachelard, the late-twentieth-century French philosopher, comments on what happens when cosmos and psyche reconnect. In the *Poetics of Space* he talks of the holy trinity of Immensity, Intensity, and Intimacy. When you have an experience of immensity—in Thomas's words, an experience of the cosmos, or a relationship to it, it is an intense experience. All awe is both an intense and intimate experience. Humans cannot separate the immense, intense, and intimate experience, and Thomas Berry, by leading us into a cosmic awareness again— an awareness as important for our hearts as for our minds—is bathing us anew in Immensity, Intensity, and Intimacy far beyond any mere anthropocentric relationship could ever do for us.

Bachelard declares that "grandeur progresses in the world in proportion to the deepening of intimacy . . . a primal value." We have to take back Immensity as a primal intimate value where "we are no longer shut up in the weight of the prison of our own beings." The new cosmology helps us to do this and so do solitude and meditation. I honor Thomas and Aquinas and others who are helping us to name the vastness of our souls. Ernest Holmes put it this way: "Spirituality is a word that is often misused." He said this one hundred years ago! "From our viewpoint, spirituality is one's recognition of the universe as a living presence of the good, truth, beauty, peace, power and love." Holmes recognizes that spirituality is not spirituality if it is psychologized—if it is not about the universe. Holmes was right and Thomas Berry is right.

Thomas Berry carries us into diversity as well. Many Western philosophers have fought over the issue of the one versus the many but neither Aquinas nor Thomas Berry is the least bit in doubt about the resolution. Many times I've heard Berry quote Aquinas on exactly this issue of the wealth of diversity. Berry calls the universe the primary artist. "In every phase of our imaginative, aesthetic, and emotional lives we are profoundly dependent on this larger context of the surrounding world." The tragedy of the ecological crisis is a soul crisis because we have been gifted with so much. Aquinas says: "Because the divine goodness could not be adequately expressed by one creature alone, God has produced many and diverse creatures so what is wanting in one in the representation of divine goodness might be supplied by another. Thus the whole universe together participates in the divine goodness. . . ."[20] So the celebration of diversity is honored in both Aquinas and Berry's thinking.

The sense of cosmology, looking at the whole and not the part, is intrinsic to all postmodern thinking but also to all premodern thinking, including Aquinas and indigenous people. This is how Aquinas put it: "Divinity is better represented by the whole universe than by any single thing. . . . Not only are individual creatures images of God but so too is the whole cosmos."[21] How many theologians or preachers have you ever heard say that—that the cosmos is an image of God? Thomas Berry says it. Berry talks about the "grand liturgy of the universe"—an image of the universe itself as a ritual—and he calls us to participate in this cosmic ritual.[22]

Aquinas says that "there is beauty in the very diversity"[23] that we find in the cosmos. In addition, he sees the universe itself as a mirror of Divinity when he observes: "God has produced a work in which the divine likeness is clearly reflected: I mean by this the world itself."[24] The world itself is a mirror of the Sacred, a mirror of Divinity, a face of God, a Christ, a Buddha, Shekinah, the Goddess—call it what you will—all that is renamed in Thomas Berry's contribution and in his celebration of beauty and diversity.

Another dimension to Berry's work that is pushed in Aquinas is that of asking the question: What is the human's role in all this? Why are we here? Aquinas says: "God wills that humans exist for the sake of the perfection of the universe." By "perfection" he means bringing to completion the tasks of the universe. Like Thomas Berry he is setting us in an ethical context of carrying on the universe's work. As Aquinas very bluntly puts it: "It is false to say that humanity is the most excellent being in the universe. The most excellent being in the universe is the universe itself." And he says "we bless God by recognizing the divine goodness."[25] If I were to pick one line for Thomas Berry's epitaph it would be that. Thomas taught us to see with new eyes (old new eyes?) the divine goodness, to see the beauty within all systems—eco, cosmic, fireball, relationship of microcosm (atoms) to macrocosm. He reseeds the goodness or blessing that is inherent in all of being. He calls us to our "Great Work."

It's interesting that many traditions of the world propose that the consequence of seeing the world cosmically and seeing it in a context of goodness is right behavior. Without this consciousness we are short on right behavior. For example, Black Elk says: "The human heart is a sanctuary at the center of which there is a little space, wherein the Great Spirit dwells, and this is the Eye. This is the Eye of the Great Spirit. . . ." Thus our cosmology becomes our ethics. Black Elk continues: "The first peace—which is the most important peace—is that which comes in the souls of people when they realize their oneness with all its powers. . . ." Thomas Berry draws us to this very teaching, that at the center of all hearts lies the center of the universe and Wanka Tanka the Holy One. If Black Elk is correct, then Thomas is an ethical teacher showing us the way to recover our peacefulness and ways of reconnecting to the powers of the universe itself.

Still another dimension to Thomas Berry's work is *intimacy,* a common word throughout his work. Aquinas put intimacy this way: "God is in all things in the most intimate way. Insofar as a thing has existence it is like God."[26] This is what Black Elk is saying: Wankan Tanka is within all things; Hildegard said "no creature lacks an intimate life." So our questing for intimacy is responded to by the yearning for intimacy from other beings of the universe and this planet. We have a right to intimacy, and things are set up biased in favor of intimacy. An anthropocentric consciousness is not capable of providing intimacy, and this is why television is run over with soap operas—an infinite amount, unending number, of pseudo-love shows that are destined not to satisfy. Intimacy is found in a more than human context, and we are invited to participate.

Another dimension to Berry's work that carries us to the next century is his profound study of deep ecumenism, which embraces the wisdom of all our religious traditions and of science itself. He brings together what has been rent asunder in the seventeenth century, science's wisdom and the potential wisdom of religion. We see in Thomas the yoga of study itself. By his lifestyle Thomas reminds us of something that our educational system has practically forgotten, and that is that learning itself is prayer. Learning itself can be a spiritual practice. The pursuit of truth is a spiritual act, a meditation. The rabbis of old knew this—studying Torah is prayer. Aquinas knew this—his study was his prayer. Our secularization of education has sucked out of us the joy and commitment and thrill and yoga that study is. The excitement and spiritual experience of learning is so often left behind. Whether one studies languages, mathematics, science, if one brings one's heart to it, it is a spiritual discipline. We thank Thomas for that, as well as Aquinas.

And finally, Thomas Berry is a true elder to the young—so important in our time. The young are yearning for elders and there are so few. What can you say of the captains of industry, the Enrons, the Andersons, the Talibans, the World Coms, the Vaticans in this moment of history? They all suffer from a terminal disease called Patriarchal Excess and from Adultism. They want to use the youth but are not there to awaken the stories of the youth. And Thomas Berry has been inspiring youth for years. The real work of the elder is to pass on stories that motivate the young to be generous and alive and use their god-given gifts to affect history so that history will not be the nightmare that Walcott named it but will be closer to that "love of the world" that it can become. Thomas Berry has done this for so many individuals.

Recently I received a letter from a twenty-two-year-old Jesuit novice who told me this story: He read my work and found Thomas Berry that way and decided to take a Greyhound bus down to North Carolina to spend a day with Thomas. "Now I know what I have to do with the rest of my life and what my generation has to do," he wrote me. That is eldership. That is the kind of effect Thomas's being and work have had and will have on countless people. I visited Earth Haven in North Carolina, an off-the-grid community, drawing very bright people to commit their lives to what is sustainable. This is the monastery of the twenty-first century. To get to the twenty-second century there will be people this generous and this alive to truly alter our ways of living on this Earth. They are beholden to Thomas Berry and his work, and Tom has visited them.

These are just two examples of Thomas Berry as elder. In effecting the relationship of young and old he is challenging everyone to grow into our role as elders and to reject our culture's heresy of "retirement" as finding the nearest golf course and squatting there until they bury you. Instead, start investing your time, wisdom, imagination, and excess money if you have some, into those movements that can make us sustainable and carry our species into a twenty-second century that will be more honorable.

If human history survives and our species survives into the twenty-second century, I believe that history will record that among us a certain prophet rose in the latter part of the twentieth century imbued with the spirit of Teilhard de Chardin, the intellect of Aquinas, the eros of Hildegard, the humility of Francis, the science of Einstein, and the courage and imagination of Jesus. His name was Thomas Berry. We will remember him by carrying on his vision, by building institutions and movements, and by infiltrating all of our professions from education to politics to business to worship with his many and sustainable visions.

4

Thomas Berry and the Evocation of Participatory Consciousness

—

Geneen Marie Haugen

To the children who swim beneath
the waves of the sea, to those who live in
the soils of the Earth.

THOMAS BERRY, *THE GREAT WORK*

There is simply no other way to begin writing about Thomas Berry and the evocation of participatory consciousness than with a bow to ancestor galaxies and blue-green bacteria, and a bow to esteemed teachers—especially to Thomas Berry himself, an uncommon man in communion with the universe, a man who was moved to dedicate books to "the children who swim beneath the waves of the sea, and to those who live in the soils of the Earth; and to the Great Red Oak, beneath whose sheltering branches these pages were written."[1] His poetic words summon forth our kinship with the Others, bring mindful our interdependence with earthly companions. By honoring the wild presences, Thomas collaborates in enlivening the world, in reawakening anima mundi from its long, human-induced sleep.

Thomas Berry's acknowledgments of the Others may seem archaic or romantically idealized to contemporary Western people, or perhaps even superfluous. But Thomas inhabited a magnificent, animated world, an ensouled universe. His offerings to the other-than-human beings were not naive, but rather, deeply informed by the body of Earth and by the cosmic mystery—and intentionally reciprocal. He expressed a consciousness of participation—as if gestures such as acknowledging the more-than-human community actually matter.

In her preface to Thomas Berry's *Evening Thoughts,* Mary Evelyn Tucker beautifully notes Berry's "pathbreaking contribution" in recognizing that human beings are "between stories—namely, between a scientific description of evolution and a Biblical account of creation."[2] In addition to apprehending that these old stories are no longer sufficient to guide us and that a new story is emerging, Thomas also discerned that these stories are not just happening *to* us, but that, aware or not, we are participants. And further, our common future depends on intentional participation. He writes, "This we need to know: how to participate creatively in the wildness of the world about us. For it is in the wild depths of the universe and our own being that the greater visions must come."[3] The visions needed to guide us are not secreted in the human creations of sciences, politics, educational systems, business institutions, or even religions, but in a far more wild—and more-than-human— terrain into which Thomas not only ventured but also participated and brought forth his own immense vision, the Great Work.

In the wild depths of the Western world, a new mode of human consciousness presses its soft prints into the ground and across the sky, leaving a scent, a faint trail for us to follow. Some have called this new mode "final participation" (Barfield), or "future participation" (Reason). For this writing I will simply call it "participatory consciousness," or a heightened, world-reshaping awareness of participation with the visible and invisible; embodied and numinous; past, present, and future beings, relationships, and energies among whom we dwell. This mode contrasts with the Cartesian bifurcation—or mind/matter and subject/ object separation—into which most Western people are indoctrinated.

It is a more porous consciousness, a felt-sense of interpenetration and reciprocity; a psychic and somatic openness to the Others and to the mysterious terrain of imagination and dream; openness to what Joanna Macy calls "deep time"—or an awareness of connection with both ancient and future beings and events.

To the Western mind participation with the nonhuman Others and with the numinous might suggest mysticism, or something unavailable to ordinary people. Yet this kind of participation is, even now, an everyday mode of being for at least some people—indigenous and others—who have not entirely succumbed to the age of reason.

In openness to deep time, this emerging mode of consciousness is not a return to our presumable primal mode of consciousness. That early mode of human consciousness was likely participatory but perhaps undifferentiated into a distinct sense of self and other, and almost certainly had no sense of what we currently understand as unrepeatable developmental movement over immense expanses of time.

Participatory consciousness emerges in relationship with an animate world, an ensouled universe with both a past and an unfolding future. Rivers and mountains, galaxies and microbes are physical and psychic presences with their own stories and longings. I believe that Thomas Berry not only expressed participatory consciousness but that he helped evoke it in others and that this evocation was one of his finest of many gifts to Earth and to the human species.

Thomas Berry did not write about the nature and evolution of "participatory consciousness" directly, in the manner of Owen Barfield, Peter Reason, and others, but he left a trail of words that helps bring into consciousness our ongoing participation: "At this moment . . . we participate in the intimacy of all things with each other."[4] And, "We renew our human participation in the grand liturgy of the universe."[5] He makes visible the web between participation and psychic vitality: "The excitement of life and the sustaining of psychic vigor are evoked by our participation in this magnificent process."[6] And he suggests that sometimes we participate in a greater dream than ours alone: "Perhaps on occasion we participate in the original dream of the earth."[7] And who can say but that Thomas Berry's participatory life was not the dream of Earth and cosmos expressing through a human being?

His assurance that the universe is a "communion of subjects"—often repeated—suggests that he *experienced* the universe as a communion, as a sacred process in which he participated. In other words, a communion of subjects was not just an idea, an abstract concept, removed from his felt-sense of the particulars of everyday life. There is no communion without participation.

Most children with access to wildish places experience deep participation and a sense of belonging to the world unless they are taught to fear nature, but for many the physical and psychic enlivening evoked by the natural world is eventually eclipsed by the demands of culture. We forget how we were once entranced by the translucent wings of butterflies, how we were transported into a magical kingdom at the sight of a deer in twilight. But Thomas Berry didn't forget. A "magic moment" at age eleven, with the lilies and the crickets and woodlands in "the meadow across the creek" profoundly informed his lifework. A seed of a lifelong project took root: "Whatever preserves and enhances this meadow in the natural cycles of its transformation is good; whatever opposes this meadow or negates it is not good." This simple, clear sense of the importance of tending the body of Earth deepened and ripened into recognition of the inherent rights and interiority of nature: "These evolving biosystems deserve the opportunity to be themselves and to express their own inner qualities." Biosystems, and the beings who comprise them, are not without their own essential natures, but rather ensouled expressions of the mystery: "We might think of a viable future for the planet . . . as participation in a symphony or as a renewed presence to some numinous presence manifested in the wonderworld about us. This was perhaps something I vaguely experienced in that first view of the lilies blooming in the meadow across the creek."[8] Once again Thomas reminds us of the necessity of participation with the great symphony of life, participation with the numinous presence glimpsed in the fantastic and wild expressions of a flourishing planet.

Not only did Thomas experience deep participation with the

phenomena of the natural world—evident in his eloquent words of communion with the night sky, rivers, mountains, and the songs of birds—he recognized, as well, that human beings participate with the universe not only bodily but also in the transmaterial realm of psyche, imagination, dream, and vision. While he often writes with heart-wrenching clarity about the perilousness of our time—as in "the human community has become a predator draining the life of its host"[9]—his language for the mysteries of psyche is often poetic, and thus his meanings are softly elusive—shifting, shading, and flaring forth, glorious, and slippery as the dawn. His language is often the language of dreams, the lexicon of a dreamer, coherent within the dream, and challenging to translate into rational thought. His is the language of a mystic: "We might say that the simplest atomic structure, the hydrogen atom, already expresses a radiant intelligibility, a psychic as well as a physical aspect of reality. It is a numinous and mystical being as well as a physical measurable being."[10] And, "Not only can two psychic forms be present to each other in the same psychic space but an unlimited number of forms can be present. Indeed, the entire universe can be present."[11]

If the entire universe can be present in the same "psychic space," then we must participate with the universe in the psychic dimension at every moment. Such conscious permeability to transmaterial dimensions might be regarded as mysticism, and Thomas Berry as a participatory mystic. Yet his attention was not directed solely to a transcendental realm, but to the *relationship* between the psychic-spiritual dimension inherent in the cosmos and the human expression of that dimension in re-creating our relationship with Earth—the "great work" of reinventing the human presence to be mutually enhancing and participatory with the earth community.

The two primary stories that have guided Western people—the biblical and scientific accounts of creation and of evolution—are lacking sufficient complexity and nuance to guide our way into what Thomas calls the Ecozoic Age. Neither story suggests the participation of human beings in the outcome of the story, as if we live in a universe where everything happens *to* us. Thomas notes that a profound reorientation has emerged. He writes: "A decisive transformation has taken place. The human had nothing to say in the emergent period of the universe before the present. In the future, however, the human will be involved in almost everything that happens."[12]

The human species already is involved in altering the biosphere whether or not we allow awareness of our actions. Much of the human community, it would seem, unconsciously participates in the unraveling of life systems by "improving" our own position of comfort in the world to the detriment of even our own kind, as well as the other-than-human communities. We helplessly follow the life-brutalizing directives of our invented economic systems "unable or unwilling to recognize . . . that our entire modern world is . . . inspired by a distorted dream experience, perhaps by the most powerful dream that has ever taken possession of the human imagination. Our sense of progress, our entire technological society . . . is a pure dream vision in its origin and in its objectives."[13]

Thomas traces the human-caused harm to our glorious world to its origin in a distorted—and unexamined—dream, its origin in a trans-material dimension of the human experience. Thus, he suggests an intrinsic intertwining of transmaterial and physical realities: "There is, I propose, an unbroken continuity in the creative process through this expanse of universe development. Both in our physical and in our psychic constitution, we are totally involved in that single vast creative process that reaches across all the distances of space and from the beginning of time to the present."[14]

Even psyche is "totally involved" in the unfolding story. Human dreams, even distorted dreams, are participatory in the story of Earth. Our distorted dream experience, our technological rapture, our unexamined faith in "progress" have brought us to the perilous edge, but it is also true that our technologies and faith in progress have given us the very tools to tune in to the cosmic unfolding. Would we know what we know of the universe story without our sophisticated instruments that look backward in time or into the beings we call cells and atoms, or without our certainty that we are entitled to expand our knowledge and our presence in the galaxy? And yet our dream of technological and scientific progress has missed attending, or finding coherence with, the mystery that interpenetrates phenomena. Thomas writes, "The new origin story, the supreme achievement of the scientific effort of these centuries, must be completed by a sense of the psychic, as well as the physical, dimensions of the evolutionary process from the beginning."[15] Until only recently we have probed the physical universe as if it is devoid of psyche, as if the imagination and curiosity of human beings do not reflect imagination and curiosity inherent in the cosmos.

If psyche or consciousness interpenetrates the phenomenal universe, who can say with certainty that our sophisticated instruments and observations were the only way we could have encountered the story of cosmic evolution? Although Thomas wrote of the importance of entering the dream or shamanic realms to find a guiding vision, it seems that he did not explore the possibility that the carbon atoms with capacity to "enter the processes of thinking"[16] might themselves be communicating with us, telling us the story of their own long journey, just beyond the reach of our ordinary perceptions.

Western minds chose to attempt to penetrate matter, but earlier and contemporary indigenous people have chosen to enter other dimensions of reality through the doorways of consciousness itself, assisted by plants—our distant kin and teachers—or by vision-evoking methods such as fasting, dancing, or a wilderness solo. The ancestral totem poles of the American Northwestern people suggest the lineage of nonhuman Others from whom a tribe descended; other tribes of this continent commonly refer to Earth, Sun, or Moon as Grandmother or Grandfather. Australian Aborigines listen for ancestor spirits in the dreaming of Earth. The recognition of reciprocity with the other-than-human community and lineage of ancestors is deeply embedded in at least some traditional peoples—a participatory relationship that yet eludes most Westerners despite our intellectual knowledge of ecological kinship. The question is not only how did people without silicon-based technology *know,* but how did they know so deeply—in a way that infused their very manner of being, in a consciousness of participation with ancestors and kin, in an ensouled and animate world?

We Westerners have benefited greatly from science—who does not tremble at the sublimely surreal photographs from the Hubble?—but what depths of experience and ways of knowing have we lost by exploring matter devoid of psyche, by severing the body from the dream? Dreams live in the same mysterious terrain as imagination, visionary experience, and psychic realities—a terrain to which Thomas points, or writes from, again and again, opening an awareness that these trans-material realms are themselves expressions of the cosmos, finding particular shape in the human.

Our special manner of dreaming[17] includes not only self-reflexive consciousness and "a special power over the universe in its earthly expression"[18]—even to the point of undermining life systems—but also our ability to imagine, dream, and envision.

The human species, as far as we know, is the only earthly creature with both an ability to envision alternate futures—dream visions that do not yet exist, possibilities that have never existed—and then to create them. The human imagination has birthed violins, spaceships, global communication, and nuclear weapons; yet we remain largely unaware of the great mystery of imagination itself and of the planetary transformations unleashed by that imagination.

The threshold crossing from unconscious participation to conscious participation—not only in our material expression but also in our psychic, imaginative expression—is an evolutionary movement that accompanies the new story.

Thomas wrote extensively and eloquently about the need to transform the human presence into a mutually enhancing relationship with Earth and cosmos, to reshape our political, economic, religious, and educational institutions to reflect our embeddedness with the rest of life. The seed from which such metamorphoses emerge is a transformed and transforming consciousness, participating with the physical and invisible presences among whom we abide. He writes, "Numinous and cosmic, as well as primordial human, forces are available in guiding the process of human development if only we will become sensitive to this guidance."[19]

Primordial, numinous, and cosmic forces may be discernable only to the transrational consciousness, the very mode of consciousness that one enters at night, sailing forth into dreams, and in wakeful visionary experience or mystical perception. When we become sensitive to this guidance and act upon it, we become conscious participants in the cosmic unfolding—familiar terrain for the shaman, who journeys "into the far regions of the cosmic mystery and brings back the vision and the power needed by the human community. . . . The shamanic personality speaks and best understands the language of the various creatures of the earth. Not only is the shamanic personality emerging in our society, but also the shamanic dimension of the psyche itself."[20]

The shamanic dimension of psyche is a primordial creature made of fur and feathers, seedpods and stardust—an unruly being who participates with the wild depths of the universe, howls with the invisible and visible Others, and dances with numinous and cosmic forces. The shamanic dimension of psyche circles and beds down, waiting, so near, just beyond the gate of our ordinary minds.

Thomas Berry did not tell us directly how to cultivate a consciousness of participation, but again and again, he shows us. Speaking to a gathering in 2000, he said: "I would suggest that we go outside this building, that we go beyond all the light and noise of the city and look up at the sky overarching the Earth. . . . We would see the stars begin to appear as the sun disappears over the horizon. . . . A stillness, a healing quiet, comes over the landscape. It is a moment when some other world makes itself known, some numinous presence beyond human understanding. We experience the wonder of things as the vast realms of space overwhelm the limitations of our human minds."[21]

He suggests that we participate in the "great liturgy of the universe"[22] by attending the transitional moments, the dawn and the mysterious twilight, the seasonal changes, the awe-filled hours of birth and death.

As I write, late in the afternoon, totally engrossed with the words on a screen, I jump up, suddenly aware that I have nearly missed the deepening pink sky, the slow darkening to lavender and purple. I run outside barefoot with a wooden flute and play a simple melody for the sky and sandstone, for the pinyon and any creatures who might hear during this snow-blanketed winter twilight. It is a kind of vesper. At other times, the flute accompanies the Moon, or the Milky Way, or the dawn. It is a kind of prayer. It is a soft song added to the great symphony of life.

A practice of celebrating the wild Earth and cosmos—like other practices—holds the possibility of reshaping consciousness; the more our thoughts, words, and gestures are intertwined with the beings among whom we abide, the more the world pulses with life, the more we hear the exuberantly singing Earth, and perhaps even the songs of starlight. Thomas wrote, "As we recover our awareness of the universe as a communion of subjects, a new interior experience awakens within the human. The barriers disappear. An enlargement of soul takes place."[23]

With an enlargement of soul, with a new interior experience, we are no longer who we were. A new participation with the world begins to emerge, sending forth simple music, listening for the voices of rivers and clouds, carbon atoms and Moon, with numinous antenna attuned to the great dreaming of Earth and cosmos.

5

Inscendence—The Key to the Great Work of Our Time

A Soulcentric View of Thomas Berry's Work

Bill Plotkin

Thomas Berry told us that in order to invent new sustainable human cultures we must root our efforts not in our rational minds but in revelatory visions that sprout from the depths of the human psyche and from our encounters with the mysteries of the natural world. He coined the word *inscendence* to refer to this descent to soul that, with good fortune, ignites visionary experience, which in turn guides transformational action. After several decades studying the traditions and religions of peoples throughout the world, Thomas concluded that culture-improving measures sourced in any of our existing traditions would be insufficient as a response to the exigencies of the twenty-first century. He advised us that solutions fabricated with our rational minds arise from the very worldviews and values that produced our current planet-wide impasse in the first place.

If Thomas was correct—and I believe he was—then we must not only question everything about our contemporary Western cultures but also reconsider much that is believed, even among our most progressive thinkers, about how to extract ourselves from our current culture-caused catastrophes. When Thomas spoke about the necessity of "reinventing the human—at the species level," he truly meant just that and not something less, such as rationally designing healthier versions of the cultures we already have. He called upon us to remake *ourselves,* not just our economies, governments, educational methods, religions, and energy-producing technologies. Thomas exhorted us to return to the original psychic and ritual processes by which healthy cultures come into existence and sustain themselves. He provocatively suggested that doing so requires "the shamanic dimension of the psyche itself."

Thomas discussed these things most explicitly and thoroughly in the title chapter of his watershed 1988 book, *The Dream of the Earth.* Significantly, this chapter's subtitle, "Our Way into the Future," is the very phrase he chose again to subtitle his subsequent book, *The Great Work,* and it is the title he selected for the first chapter of *Evening Thoughts.* Here's the extraordinary paragraph in which he wrote of inscendence:

> [W]e must go far beyond any transformation of contemporary culture. We must go back to the genetic imperative from which human cultures emerge originally and from which they can never be separated without losing their integrity and their survival capacity. None of our existing cultures can deal with this situation out of its own resources. We must invent, or reinvent, a sustainable human culture by a descent into our pre-rational, our instinctive resources. Our cultural resources have lost their integrity. They cannot be trusted. What is needed is not transcendence but "inscendence," not the brain but the gene.[1]

I want to explore here what Thomas meant by inscendence, its relationship to "the dream of the Earth," why he felt the "descent into our pre-rational, our instinctive resources" is critically important, and how it contrasts with and complements other, more infrastructural approaches to cultural change. Then I want to inquire into his use of the phrase "the genetic imperative" and thereby throw into relief his view of the relationship between nature, soul, and culture. Finally, I want to investigate one of Thomas's signature phrases, "the spontaneities within us," how these spontaneities can guide us, and their relationship with inscendence and soul.

It's not a coincidence I've chosen to write about this "inscendental" (but not in the least incidental) dimension of Thomas's work. The descent to soul has been the central theme of my own writing and the goal of the wilderness experiences in which I have guided others for thirty years. During my interview with Thomas in March 2006, I was particularly intent on learning more about what he meant by inscendence and what techniques he recommended for evoking this experience. His response took me by surprise: "I mean the work you do, Bill." Although disappointed, I wasn't likely to learn more about his view of inscendence beyond what he had already written, I was also both honored and gratified that he understood my efforts in this way. (Thomas's awareness of my work derived from my 2003 book, *Soulcraft,* for which he wrote the foreword.)

INSCENDENCE AND THE DREAM OF THE EARTH

In his books, what did Thomas tell us about inscendence?

In *The Dream of the Earth,* Thomas called for a new "cultural coding," which I have understood to mean root patterns, seed ideas, or consciousness-shifting images that might animate healthy, creative, sustainable cultures of the future. And he told us exactly where to find such catalysts.

> The new cultural coding that we need must emerge from the source of all such codings, from revelatory vision that comes to us in those special psychic moments, or conditions, that we describe as "dream." We are, of course, using this term not only as regards the psychic processes that take place when we are physically asleep, but also as

a way of indicating an intuitive, nonrational process that occurs when we awaken to the numinous powers ever present in the phenomenal world about us, powers that possess us in our high creative moments. Poets and artists continually invoke these spirit powers, which function less through words than through symbolic forms.[2]

We need to remember that this process whereby we invent ourselves in these cultural modes is guided by visionary experiences that come to us in some transrational process from the inner shaping tendencies that we carry within us, often in revelatory dream experience.[3] This intimacy with our genetic endowment, and through this endowment with the larger cosmic process, is . . . the role of the shamanic personality, a type that is emerging once again in our society.

More than any other of the human types concerned with the sacred, the shamanic personality journeys into the far reaches of the cosmic mystery and brings back the vision and the power needed by the human community at the most elementary level.[4] Consider, then, the following phrases as Thomas's composite definition of inscendence:

- "a descent into our pre-rational, our instinctive resources"
- "revelatory vision that comes to us in . . . 'dream'" [whether we are asleep or awake]
- "an intuitive, nonrational process that occurs when we awaken to the numinous powers ever present in the phenomenal world about us"
- "visionary experiences that come to us in some transrational process from the inner shaping tendencies that we carry within us, often in revelatory dream experience"
- "journeys into the far reaches of the cosmic mystery [to bring] back the vision and the power needed by the human community at the most elementary level"

To distill even further, we might say that Thomas's inscendence is a conscious connecting with any of the following: "instinctive resources," "revelatory dream experience," "vision," our own "inner shaping tendencies," "the numinous powers of the phenomenal world," or the "cosmic mystery." Quite a list! What do they have in common?

First of all, these are the realms of human experience most ignored by the mainstream in Western and Westernized cultures. Interesting and—not a coincidence. Mass culture labels these realms "mystical," often with a pejorative or disdainful connotation and with an attitude of superiority. In contrast, many nature-based traditions and our own innate human intuition tell us these realms dwell at the very heart of the world, at the very core of life, that they centrally inform our humanity. Indeed, these are the dwelling places of the sacred.

Second, all of Thomas's instances of inscendence lie outside the realm of what the conscious mind controls. Inscendence occurs when human consciousness makes contact with and is transformed by a mystery beyond its own ken. The key to our survival and evolution, Thomas told us, lies not in our consciousness but in our conscious connection with what lies beneath it.

There's also one apparent *lack* of unity among these realms of experience. They straddle what conventional Western science and philosophy consider a definitive divide, an uncrossable border. The first four (instinct, dream, vision, shaping tendencies) would be deemed, by dualistic thinking, as "inner" and the final two (the phenomenal world, the cosmos) as "outer." But wait. The first four are more accurately identified as qualities of the person (not *in* the person) and the latter two are of the world (and not at all independent of the observing person). All of them are *in the world*.

In other words, the experience of inscendence, which Thomas said is our source for new cultural codings, can occur through our deep imagination and also through our capacities of perception. For example, we can encounter the numinous—the sacred or holy—in dreams (one mode of the deep imagination), and we can encounter it in the "phenomenal world about us." This is to say that the numinous is as much a dimension of the human as it is of the world more generally. The dream of the earth lives in and through us as much as it does in and through the rest of creation. We can access the earth's dreaming psychologically (intrapsychically) as surely as we can perceive with our senses how the dream of the earth permeates all of terrestrial nature. As Thomas reminded us, the human is part and parcel of this world, not an alien visitor. Indeed he wrote that we are "a mode of being of the universe as well as distinctive beings in the universe."[5] We are "that reality in whom the entire Earth comes to a special mode of reflexive consciousness. We are ourselves a mystical quality of the Earth, a unifying principle, an integration of the various polarities of the material and the spiritual, the physical and the psychic, the natural and the artistic, the intuitive and the scientific."[6]

The Cartesian cleaving of spirit from matter, mind from body, and inner from outer—that partitioning of the world and ourselves into pairs of disparate domains—is one way Western culture has undermined our full experience of the reality of both ourselves and the world in which we live. But we no longer need think or talk this way. We no longer need to separate ourselves from the world. We no longer need to de-soul the world. It's high time we returned home, to once again participate fully in what Thomas called a "communion of subjects," the Earth community, in which "every organism [is] by definition an ensouled being."[7]

A third motif running through Thomas's composite definition of *inscendence* is his insistence that our primary path to healthy human culture is *not* by means of our rationality. "Our way into the future" cannot be identified by our strategic minds, cannot be discerned through our capacity for deduction, our ability to figure it out, or to rationally agree upon a reasonable course of action. Even blue-ribbon panels of the best minds of our generation are not going to save us.

Accepting this limit to our rationality might feel like a blow to our human pride. After all, our rationality is a good candidate for what distinguishes us as human. So we confront here an irony arising like a specter or a terrifying god from the very core of our existence: Our human rationality is not what *made* us human and will not by itself enable us to correct our course or become *better* humans. Our rationality itself comes from somewhere other than our rationality. We did not invent ourselves. And we cannot rationally *reinvent* ourselves—at least not a healthy, sustainable version of ourselves. But we can, Thomas told us, reinvent ourselves nonrationally. And we must.

Our rational, strategic minds are designed (brilliantly) for implementation, for making things happen, for fashioning the tools, edifices, social practices, and institutions of our daily lives. Our strategic minds, in short, determine *how* to do things. But they are not designed for determining *what* is truly worthwhile to do in life. The latter is the role of what Thomas referred to as our "inner shaping tendencies" or, as we shall see, the "human soul" or the "spontaneities within us."

This is what I hear Thomas saying when he writes that healthy cultural codings derive from what he calls "our genetic coding," not from our rational minds, not from "the brain." Inscendence is a route to the "pre-rational," the "nonrational," or the "transrational." He says it all three ways. For us to survive as (rational) humans, we must seek guidance from something that comes before our rationality, or that transcends it: "If we will the future effectively it will be because the guidance and the powers of the Earth have been communicated to us, not because we have determined the future of the Earth simply with some rational faculty."[8] This last sentence is well worth reading at least twice, perhaps even posting above our desks, in our job descriptions, and at the entrance to our universities, especially by those of us who believe we can simply reason our way out of our current dilemmas. This applies to deep ecologists, socialists, green-industry promoters, and peace activists as much as it does to true believers in capitalism, "just wars," and technological fixes.

Rather than with our rationality, the way we rediscover the earth's dream for the human (or receive an update on this ever-evolving dream) is, Thomas wrote, through our own capacity to dream. When we are physically asleep, we refer to such experiences simply as dreams, but when we are awake, we might speak of visions or numinous experiences or, as I prefer, encounters with the soul or encounters with the great mystery (Thomas's "cosmic mystery").

It is only by means of revelatory vision that we can nourish or revitalize our full humanity. And only by becoming fully human do we participate wholly in the dream of the Earth—Earth's dream for itself, which is Earth's way of participating in the dream of the universe.

Conversely, when we collectively lose touch with the dream of the Earth, we become estranged from our human destiny and become "the affliction of the world, its demonic presence,"[9] a "destructive pathology"[10] on this planet. Eventually we reach a terminal condition, the one in which we now in fact find ourselves: a terrestrial presence that threatens the survival of most of Earth's life-forms. Suicidal, biocidal, geocidal.

Thomas asked, rhetorically, "How and why did our present devastation of the Earth happen?"[11] His answer was *transcendence*—in fact, six transcendences. Two among these* are "a transcendent, personal, monotheistic creative deity," whose existence "tends to desacralize the phenomenal world" and suppresses or evicts "the feminine Earth-dwelling deities"; and the transcendental contention that we humans are "spiritual beings" and consequently "do not form a single society with the natural world," resulting in our tragic alienation from "the visible world."[12] Thomas, who we must remember was a Christian monk, coined the word *inscendence* to indicate our path of descent into a viable future, a path that contrasts with the transcendent trajectory ascended by Western civilization within its "biblical Christian humanist matrix."[13]

Thomas told us there are times in life when, as individuals, we must descend to our instinctive resources in order to reinvent ourselves. And there are times when our species, collectively, must do so. Now is very much such a time.

Rainer Maria Rilke concurred with the inevitability of the

---

*The other four transcendences are the belief in redemption ("we are not for this world"), the Cartesian transcendence of the mind (over matter), technology that allows us to transcend natural biological limits to our numbers, and the belief that our human destiny is in some other world.

downward spiritual journey. He turned to the metaphor of summer's end. When the easy-sailing, easy-living times naturally draw to a close, we must descend, he wrote, like tree sap going to ground in the fall.

> *The weeks stood still in summer.*
> *The trees' blood rose. Now you feel*
> *it wants to sink back*
> *into the source of everything. You thought*
> *you could trust that power*
> *when you plucked the fruit;*
> *now it becomes a riddle again,*
> *and you again a stranger.*[14]

Inscendence is this "sinking back into the source of everything," during which we must learn to trust our unknowing and during which we no longer belong to the world in our old ways, "a stranger" again. There, in the presence of "the source of everything," we hope to be suffused by and informed by what Thomas called "the guidance and the powers of the Earth."

Rilke reminded us:

> *If we surrendered*
> *to earth's intelligence*
> *we could rise up rooted, like trees.*[15]

Consider "rise up rooted, like trees" to be a fabulous image for a sustainable human culture. How do we achieve it? We begin with a descent. Doing so is as natural as falling:

> *How surely gravity's law,*
> *strong as an ocean current,*
> *takes hold of even the smallest thing*
> *and pulls it toward the heart of the world.*[16]

"Earth's intelligence"—the dream of the Earth, the pull of its numinous gravity—draws us down toward "the heart of the world." By means of this communion, we can re-member ourselves, enabling us, when ripened, to "rise up rooted, like trees."

Healthy cultures from all times and places have invented a great variety of rituals and practices to help their developmentally ready members descend to soul. Different kinds of consciousness-shifting technologies are employed as a component of these practices, ranging from fasting, trance rhythms and dancing, entheogens, dreaming, prolonged solo wandering, ceremonial sweats, breathwork, yoga, and extreme physical exertion.

Inscendence practices, in essence, support the individual to cooperate with, to surrender to, the pull of the dream of the earth, also known as the call of the soul. This descent is experienced as a psychospiritual dying. We must die to our old way of belonging to the world to enable us to uncover something radical, something new, something we could never have rationally deduced, something that our lives depend on.

For the past thirty years, my colleagues and I at Animas Valley Institute have been shaping and employing contemporary, Western, nature-based practices for inscendence. We call this work soulcraft, as described in my book of that title. But thirty years is close to nothing. For the past *hundred thousand years or more,* humans have invented and employed related methods and have told their stories of descent through the oral literature we call myths. From *Soulcraft:*

> The Greeks told the tale of Orpheus, the fabulously skilled musician who traveled to Hades to find and revive his dead bride, Eurydice. He succeeds at the rescue but then, as he leads her back to the daylight world, loses her again (and this time forever) when he disobeys the gods by turning around to make sure she is still there.
>
> Persephone, the daughter of the fertility goddess, Demeter, is abducted by Hades, the lord of the dark underworld, to be his bride. Eventually, Zeus sends Hermes to rescue Persephone (with only partial success: she must spend one-third of each year below). The

Anglo-Saxon Norsemen told the story of the hero-warrior Beowulf, who descends into a dreadful swamp to do battle with the monster of all monsters, Grendel's mother. Beowulf slays the beast but returns as part monster himself.

From the ancient Sumerian world comes the myth of the goddess of heaven, Inanna, who descends to the netherworld to confront her dark sister, the goddess Ereshkigal, who kills Inanna and hangs her corpse on a peg. Two mourners are sent to Ereshkigal by Enki, the god of waters and wisdom, and secure Inanna's release, but Inanna must send a substitute to take her place in the netherworld.

The Nubian people of Saharan Africa recount the story of a young woman who, because of her beauty, is spurned by the other women of the village. In her despair, she descends to the bottom of a river, a very dangerous place, where she encounters a repulsive old woman covered with horrible sores who asks the young woman to lick her wounds. She does and is thereby saved from the monster of the depths. She returns to the village with great gifts.

Such myths and stories are found in countless cultures. They imply we each must undertake the journey of descent if we are to heal ourselves at the deepest levels and reach a full and authentic adulthood, that there are powerful and dangerous beings in the underworld who are not particularly friendly or attractive, and that we are forever changed by the experience. In contemporary Western cultures, we live as if the spiritual descent is no longer necessary; we live without realizing that the journey is meant for each one of us, not just for the heroes and heroines of mythology.[17]

Thomas is clear that "the challenge before us . . . the historical mission of our times, is to reinvent the human—at the species level,"[18] but other changes—infrastructural modifications that can be rationally figured out—are also essential in the relative short-term. Reinventing the human by way of inscendence is going to take several generations—and each community, nation, tribe, or people that survive the twenty-first century will necessarily do it in their own distinctive way. But there are numerous societal changes that must be made in the next couple of decades. We no longer have enough time to rely on inscendence alone. Humanity must learn very soon to become a well-mannered team player in the earth community, an integral participant in the web of life, using no more than what Earth can replenish and discarding only what can be easily and safely assimilated.

We must, for example, eliminate environmental poisons, vastly improve the Western diet, minimize our use of fossil fuels, substantially decrease our need for energy, invent and implement renewable energy sources, save our remaining forests and plant new ones, radically rework the way we charter corporations, learn to educate young people in ways that enable them to take their place as contributing members of the earth community, teach government leaders the arts of negotiation and social justice (i.e., real peacemaking) and empower them to actually use these arts (for example, imagine the U.S. Congress if . . .), create better games than war, and redesign our political, judicial, and electoral systems so as to create true democracies and, eventually, biocracies.

REVELATION: FOR THE ONE OR THE MANY?

Did Thomas mean we each must individually inscend/descend, seeking a personal vision that would enable us in our unique way to help create a healthy, sustainable culture? Or did he mean that one or a few gifted individuals in each society must descend and return with a vision that can inspire and redirect an entire culture? Or both?

Most of Thomas's references to dream experience or revelatory vision seem ambiguous on this point. But there are exceptions. For instance:

> This intimacy . . . with the larger cosmic process is not primarily the role of the philosopher, priest, prophet, or professor. It is the role of the shamanic personality, a type that is emerging once again in our society.
>
> More than any other of the human types concerned with the sacred, the shamanic personality journeys into the far reaches of the

cosmic mystery and brings back the vision and the power needed by the human community at the most elementary level. The shamanic personality speaks and best understands the language of the various creatures of the earth.

So far in this passage, it seems he meant the realm of vision to be the domain or mission of the presumably rare individual in a society, the "shamanic personality." But then in the very next sentence: "Not only is the shamanic type emerging in our society, but also the shamanic dimension of the psyche itself. In periods of significant cultural creativity, this aspect of the psyche takes on a pervasive role throughout the society and shows up in all the basic institutions and professions."[19]

Whether or not the healthy societies of the past were replete with mature members who experienced and embodied revelatory vision, I believe, along with Thomas, that this is both possible and necessary in this century if we are to successfully reinvent the human. Sustainable societies, at this turning point in human and Earth's evolution, will come about through neither human rationality nor the vision of a few individuals alone but through the "pervasive" emergence of "the shamanic dimension of the psyche." Although the vision of the one can catalyze the many, the vision of each is needed to build the new cultures.

Additional indications that Thomas understood revelatory vision as the opportunity, if not the obligation, of all mature people are:

[E]ach individual is not only different from every other being in the universe but also has its own inner articulation, its unique spontaneities. Each being in its subjective depths carries that numinous mystery whence the universe emerges into being. This we might identify as the sacred depth of the individual.[20]

The natural world demands a response that rises from the wild unconscious depths of the human soul. A response that artists seek to provide in color and music and movement.[21]

Through my study of human development and visionary experience I have grown certain that every human is born with the potential and promise of the true artist. All of us have been designed by nature to mature into our full humanity as visionary artisans of cultural evolution. We are each born with a wildly creative destiny. But this birthright does not come with a guarantee of fulfillment. The realization of our individual soul identities depends largely upon the vitality of cultural practices that prepare us for the eventual experience of inscendence. When such cultural practices are forgotten or degraded, few realize their destiny—and society as a whole disintegrates and lapses into what Thomas termed a "destructive pathology."

One final distinction must be explored related to this question of revelation for the one or the many: Was Thomas calling for visions that uniquely guide individual lives, or about shared visions for guiding an entire culture? It turns out he was writing about both. But between the publications of *Dream* (1988) and *The Great Work* (1999), Thomas seems to have retreated somewhat from his emphasis on inscendence—in the sense of the precultural and prerational guidance we receive individually from dream or revelatory vision. In *The Great Work* and in *Evening Thoughts* he gave greater emphasis to the importance of collective or shared vision. For example, from *The Great Work:* "The historical mission of our times is to reinvent the human—at the species level . . . by means of story and shared dream experience."[22]

Unfortunately, he left us without an elaborate explanation of "shared dream experience." But there are sufficient clues. For example:

At such a moment [of cultural pathology] a new revelatory experience is needed, an experience wherein human consciousness awakens to the grandeur and sacred quality of the Earth process. This awakening is our human participation in the dream of the Earth.[23]

[T]he foundations of a new historical period, the Ecozoic Era, have been established in every realm of human affairs. The mythic vision has been set into place. The distorted dream of an industrial technological paradise is being replaced by the more viable dream of a mutually enhancing human presence within an ever-renewing organic-based Earth community. The dream drives the action. In the larger cultural context the dream becomes the myth that both guides and drives the action.[24]

Apparently then, by "shared dream experience" Thomas meant collectively held aspirations or ambitions, not individual inscendence that results in a revelatory vision of how to personally contribute to life, whether or not in resonance with a shared vision. He meant "mythic vision" or cultural "myth," the zeitgeist of a people, the defining spirit of a cultural era—in particular, a mythic vision ignited by our collective awakening to "the grandeur and sacred quality of the Earth process." By "story and shared dream experience," Thomas was evoking the dream of the earth, the universe story, and the vision of a new historical period he called the Ecozoic Era.

Although awakening to "the grandeur and sacred quality of the Earth process" is a transformative experience for people of Western and Westernized cultures, perhaps even a spiritual watershed and certainly a necessary component of our cultural therapy, this ecological illumination is distinct from the numinous encounter with the mysteries of one's own soul, one's particular way of participating in "the Earth process." Evoking our more general participatory consciousness—"our human participation in the dream of the Earth"—is what Thomas meant by our awakening to "the grandeur and sacred quality of the Earth process." This "dream of a mutually enhancing human presence within an ever-renewing organic-based Earth community" arises not from inscendence but from sustained experiential immersion in the more-than-human world. It also arises from simply being raised in a nature-based culture, or from participation in rituals rooted in an appreciation of the sacredness of nature's forms and rhythms, or from how the ecological stories, myths, and perspectives communicated by awakened others resonate with and arouse our own innate intuitions of our full membership in the earth community—both the joys and obligations thereof.

The urgency of "revelatory vision that comes to us in those special psychic moments, or conditions, that we describe as 'dream'" seems to receive less emphasis from Thomas after *Dream*. But instances of inscendence are not entirely absent in *The Great Work*. For example: "The architect who looked out over the fields south of Paris and saw, through the mist of the future, the Chartres Cathedral must have experienced a moment when the wild and the sacred came together in a single moment of vision."[25]

"Moment[s] when the wild and the sacred [come] together in a single moment of vision": here we have another evocative characterization of inscendence.

"THE GENETIC IMPERATIVE"

Beginning no later than *Dream* and continuing through his later essays, Thomas referred often to genetics. In particular, as we've seen, he distinguished between our "genetic coding" and our "cultural coding." He noted that to become fully human, we've always depended, since the opening of the human story, on the guidance of both kinds of codings. He emphasized, however, that our genetic coding is primary and foundational and that our cultural codings—our "cultural traditions"[26]—are derivative of our genetic coding. In particular, he was ardent that in recent centuries our Western cultural codings have lost so much of their integrity that we must now fully turn to "the genetic imperative from which human cultures emerge originally."

I want to explore here what Thomas meant by "genetic coding," because I believe it is something rather more psychological, spiritual, and mysterious than what biologists intend by the phrase. In particular, I believe Thomas meant what might be more accurately and aptly referred to as *the human soul's code,* which is, in essence, nature's design for our species, or what I've come to call our *nature coding.* When referring to genes, Thomas was thinking, writing, and speaking as an eco-theologian and as a mystic, not as a natural scientist. Many contemporary people, especially scientists, might be confused or misled by Thomas's references to genetics. An attempt at clarification is in order.

Let's take a look at how Thomas elaborated upon his understanding of genetics.

> The genetic coding that gives to the human its species identity is integral with this larger complex of codings whereby the universe exists, whereby the earth system remains coherent within itself and capable of continuing the evolutionary process. To remain viable a species must establish a niche for itself that is beneficial both for itself and for the surrounding community. The difficulty generally with this proposal is that our genetic endowment is considered to be a mere physical determination of our being, not also our richest psychic endowment, our guiding and inspiring force, especially when the cultural process has entered into a destructive pathology.[27]

For Thomas, then, our "genetic coding" gives shape to our psyches as much as it does to our bodies; it enables us to establish an ecological niche for ourselves in dynamic partnership with other species; and, most significantly, *it guides and inspires us*. I am struck by the fact that this is much the way we depth psychologists speak of the soul. The possibility that this is in fact how Thomas, too, understood "genetic coding" is further revealed in the following passage: "We must find our primary source of guidance in the inherent tendencies of our genetic coding. These tendencies are derived from the larger community of the Earth and eventually from the universe itself. In Jungian terms, these tendencies identify with those psychic energy constellations that take shape as the primary archetypal forms deep in the unconscious realms of the human. Such forms find expression in the symbols of the Heroic Journey, Death-Rebirth, the Sacred Center, the Great Mother, the Tree of Life."[28]

If the "inherent tendencies of our genetic coding . . . *identify with* [my emphasis] . . . archetypal forms deep in the unconscious realms of the human," then Thomas's "gene" might as well identify with the soul. Put even more clearly and explicitly: "Through the archetypal symbols of the unconscious, the symbols of the Great Journey, Death-Rebirth, the Cosmic Tree, and the Sacred Center we establish vital contact with those underlying energies that guide and sustain the human soul. These energies find expression especially in our dreams."[29]

Having thereby closed the gap between the soul and his conception of genetics, Thomas next integrates soul and nature more generally: "Through these symbols, interior energies that sustain the human venture and the entire civilizational process are renewed. Ultimately these symbols reflect the powers of the Earth both in their ever-renewing seasonal significance and in their irreversible evolutionary transformations."[30]

I invite you to carefully examine these statements with me: Thomas held that the "inherent tendencies of our genetic coding . . . identify with" the unconscious "archetypal forms," which are symbols that "guide and sustain the human soul," "renew the human venture," and "reflect the powers of the Earth." For Thomas, our "genetic imperative" is, in essence, the soul's guidance. And clearly for Thomas (as for me), the human soul is an element or dimension or mode of the earth itself and emerges therefrom. The realms of the soul and nature are coextensive. And both function in part through what Thomas referred to as our "genetic endowment," a phrase which we can now understand that he used in an eco-psychological way or, indeed, as a concept of what I have come to call eco-depth psychology.

In my view, to speak of the collective human soul is to speak of the place that humans occupy as a species in the ecology of Earth—or are at least *meant* to occupy. The function of a healthy culture is to support humans to occupy their proper and authentic ecological niche and to do so sustainably, gracefully, and imaginatively—perhaps even beautifully—which is to say, in mutually beneficial compatibility with other species. As Thomas put it, "To remain viable a species must establish a niche for itself that is beneficial both for itself and for the surrounding community." A healthy culture enables us "to be present to the Earth in a mutually enhancing manner."[31] A culture that fails to do so has entered "a deep cultural pathology"[32] or "a profound cultural disorientation."[33] At such times, Thomas counsels, we must look for primary guidance, not from our own traditions or those of any other culture, but from the realm of dream—both individual revelatory vision and the greater dream of the earth.

How do we access the dream of the earth? Thomas's three main suggestions are: through individual revelation, through the archetypes of the human unconscious, and in the stories of the earth and the universe. The latter stories are revealed to us through modern science when its findings are embraced in their full spiritual and mystical significance ("where human consciousness awakens to the grandeur and sacred quality of the Earth process").[34]

We must note that by the word *universe,* Thomas does not mean anything like a Newtonian mechanism, a mere "collection of objects," but rather, as mentioned, a self-organizing "communion of subjects" resulting from an extraordinarily creative process. The universe itself, Thomas writes, "seems to be the fulfillment of something so highly imaginative and so overwhelming that it must have been dreamed into existence."[35]

As an additional indication that Thomas understood genetics through a much larger lens than most biologists, and the universe more holistically and mystically than most scientists, notice that he saw the reach of "genetics" extending well beyond earthly life: "The universe is a unity, an interacting and genetically related community of beings bound together in an inseparable relationship in space and time.[36] The etymological root of *genetics* is *gen,* which means "kin." In this sense, "genetically related" is somewhat redundant: "related as kin." The root *gen* also means "that which produces." So when Thomas wrote, "We must go back to the genetic imperative from which human cultures emerge originally," he might as well have said, "We must go back to that which produces human culture originally," which begs the question: Well, what *does* produce human culture originally? I prefer Thomas's answers: "the powers of the Earth" or "the dream of the Earth." To me, these answers are much more appealing, meaningful, and actionable compared to "our genetic coding."

My reading is that Thomas understood "genetic coding" to actually be part of the means by which the souls of living beings (and thereby the earth) function. This seems to be revealed, for example, in one of his remarkable, lyrical passages from *The Great Work*. He wrote that anyone who has wondered about "the stars, the ocean, the song and flight of birds, the exquisite form and activities of the various animal species, or the awesome views of the mountains and rivers and valleys" must have

> some sense of an inner spontaneity, a guiding principle, a consciousness, a transmaterial presence manifested throughout the material embodiment, an ordering principle observed in any living being that enables the complexity of the DNA in the genetic process to function in some coherent fashion. While no sense faculty can experience it directly and no equation can be written to express it, our immediate perception tells us that there is a unifying principle in the acorn that enables the complex components of the genetic coding of the oak tree to function as a unity—send down roots, raise the trunk, extend the branches and put forth leaves and fashion its seeds, then to nourish all this by drawing up tons of water and minerals from the Earth and distributing them throughout the entire life system. That such a vast complexity of functioning should have some unifying principle, known traditionally as the "soul" of the organism, is immediately evident to human intelligence.[37]

In other words, it is the soul—"the unifying principle" of a living being—that, in Thomas's view, enables the gene "to function in some coherent manner." In addition to enabling the gene, the soul guides a living thing in part *through* the functioning of the gene. Genetics was employed by Thomas as one part of an explanation of how the soul operates. But, as Thomas implicated in the above paragraph, the soul is primary, the gene a means for the soul's embodiment, a means enabled by the soul itself. The gene is an agent of the soul, an agent capacitated by the soul. The gene, as a biological concept, helps to explain how; it does not tells us what actually happens or why.*

Now perhaps we can more fully appreciate the relationships that Thomas elucidated between human revelatory experience, the dream of the earth, and what he referred to as our "genetic coding." In the following passage, he encapsulates these relationships. As you read this you might join me, if you'd like, in substituting "souls" for "genetic coding."

> At such a moment [of profound cultural disorientation] a new revelatory experience is needed, an experience wherein human consciousness awakens to the grandeur and sacred quality of the Earth process. This awakening is our human participation in the dream of the Earth, the dream that is carried in its integrity not in any of Earth's cultural expressions but in the depths of our genetic coding. Therein the Earth functions at a depth beyond our capacity for active thought. We can only be sensitized to what is being revealed to us. We probably have not had such participation in the dream of the Earth since earlier shamanic times, but therein lies our hope for the future for ourselves and for the entire Earth community.[38]

Our participation in the dream of the earth—by way of revelatory experience, or inscendence—offers our only long-term hope for the future. The dream of the Earth, after all, is the matrix from which we originally emerged as a species. We must now return to these roots. Note, too, that Thomas emphasized again in this passage that the dream of the Earth is not something we can deduce or figure out. It is "beyond our capacity for active thought." It is either revealed to us (by the earth itself or by our souls), or we do not come to know it at all.

---

*In another, later essay, Thomas defines *soul* as "the primary organizing, sustaining, and guiding principle of a living being." This appears to be an elaboration and further differentiation of "unifying principle." (From his foreword to *Soulcraft*.)

"THE SPONTANEITIES WITHIN US"

Among the uncommon words Thomas liked to commonly use, one of my favorites is *spontaneities*. In its first appearance in his "Dream of the Earth" chapter, Thomas wrote that our genetic coding guides us "throughout the entire course of our existence, a guidance manifested through the spontaneities within us."[39] By exploring what Thomas meant by *spontaneities,* we might reach a deeper understanding yet of Thomas's concepts of "genetic coding" and "the dream of the Earth" and how they guide us.

But first a necessary interlude: Thomas emphasized that our genetic coding is not actually our only source of guidance in the absence of healthy cultures. He identified two other realms with scope and significance even greater than our genes.

> Beyond our genetic coding, we need to go to the earth, as the source whence we came, and ask for its guidance, for the earth carries the psychic structure as well as the physical form of every living being upon the planet. Our confusion is not only within ourselves; it concerns also our role in the planetary community. Even beyond the earth, we need to go to the universe and inquire concerning the basic issues of reality and value, for, even more than the earth, the universe carries the deep mysteries of our existence within itself. We cannot discover ourselves without first discovering the universe, the earth, and the imperatives of our own being.[40]

By implication, this last item, "the imperatives of our own being," must be a reference to "our genetic coding," but by denotation, the phrase seems much closer to "the spontaneities within us"—indeed nearly a synonym, but with an added sense of urgency. This is one reason I say it's actually these spontaneities, not our genetic coding, that are the primary phenomena of guidance found within the human sphere—and that Thomas understood it this way, too. But there are other reasons for this conclusion. For example, let's ask: How exactly do we "go to" our genetic coding for guidance? Is this accomplished the same way we go to the Earth or the universe?

First, the Earth: Much of Thomas's writing and teaching inspires us to be guided directly and experientially by the Earth—to open our senses, feelings, imagination, and thinking to the "wonder and grandeur of life."[41] One example:

> Only if the human imagination is activated by the flight of the great soaring birds in the heavens, by the blossoming flowers of Earth, by the sight of the sea, by the lightning and thunder of the great storms that break through the heat of the summer, only then will the deep inner experiences be evoked within the human soul.
>
> All these phenomena of the natural world fling forth to the human a challenge to be responded to in literature, in architecture, ritual, and art, in music and dance and poetry. The natural world demands a response beyond that of rational calculation, beyond philosophical reasoning, beyond scientific insight. The natural world demands a response that rises from the wild unconscious depths of the human soul. A response that artists seek to provide in color and music and movement.[42]

Here Thomas gives us a gorgeously expressed instance of how Earth guides us by way of our imagination, feeling, and sensing. But Earth also guides us through a blend of our careful sensing and thinking. For instance, by observing closely the ways each Earth creature is in relationship to the others in its environment and to the Sun, Moon, plants, waters, landforms, and air, we can (and do) learn much about our own "role in the planetary community." And in offering our imaginative attention to the nonhuman world, we sometimes catch the wind of a story unfolding there—a story that might eventually evolve into a myth—a tale that offers profound guidance for our human lives.

Earth also guides us directly by way of the other animals, those who appear to us when we are awake and those we encounter in our dreams. Sometimes animals show us the way home, teach us about healing plants, or give us songs to learn and sing. They show us how to renew our fragmented world. Plants sometimes guide us, too, in both our dayworlds and nightworlds, as does the wind, which connects us to all other creatures.

And how does the universe guide us? The answer is at the very core of Thomas's lifework and can be found throughout his writings. For example: "The greatest single need for the survival of the Earth or of the human community in the twenty-first century is for an integral telling of the great story of the universe. This story must provide in our times what the mythic stories of earlier times provided as the guiding and energizing sources of the human venture." And: "The three basic tendencies of the universe at all levels of reality are differentiation, spontaneous self-organization, and bonding. These tendencies identify the reality, the values, and the directions in which the universe is proceeding."[43]

It seems clear enough, then, how the Earth and the universe guide us. But what about our genetic coding? How do we seek *its* guidance? Are we to analyze the sequencing of our DNA to gain ecological, cultural, psychological, or spiritual direction? Would the microbiological details of our genetic code tell us how to proceed in creating a sustainable culture? I think not. I don't believe Thomas had in mind anything so literal, biological, or objective. In whatever way our genetic coding physiologically influences or shapes us (can we even really say "guides" us?), it certainly doesn't provide us direction in the same sense that the Earth and universe do.

Apparently, Thomas understood it this way, too. When it comes to how our genetic coding guides us, he suggested we attend not to DNA sequencing but to the "spontaneities within us," which *"carry out"** the guidance of our genes:

---

*"Carry out" are his words, but my emphasis. From *Dream*, 196: "the organic functioning that takes place in our sense functions; . . . our capacity for transforming food into energy; . . . our thought, imaginative, and emotional life . . . healing whenever we sustain any physical injury . . . [the capacity to] experience joy and sorrow . . . the ability to speak and think and create . . . the context of our relation with the divine. All this is carried out by the spontaneities within us."

We have ultimately no other source of guidance [other than these spontaneities] that possesses such inherent authenticity or which can function so effectively as a norm of reference in our actions. In earlier times these spontaneities were considered as revealing the natural law, the ultimate inner norm of guidance for human conduct, since they are the human phase of those instincts that enable a bird to build its nest, find its food, and discover its migratory route. Ultimately these instincts come from that mysterious source from where the universe itself came into being as articulated entities acting together in some ordered context.[44]

Thomas's "spontaneities within us," then, are our instinctive human ways of perceiving, thinking, feeling, imagining, speaking, and acting—ways of knowing and behaving that are not rationally deducted or consciously chosen but come to us "naturally."*

Notice, too, that if our spontaneities are our instincts, and if inscendence is "a descent into our pre-rational, our instinctive resources," then inscendence is a way to identify and reclaim the spontaneities within us. This is why, for Thomas, inscendence is our means to "invent, or reinvent, a sustainable human culture."

In his discussion of cultural transformation, the particular human instinct, or spontaneity, that Thomas highlighted is "dream vision": "The dream comes about precisely through the uninhibited spontaneities of which we are speaking. In this context we might say: In the beginning was the dream. Through the dream all things were made, and without the dream nothing has been made that has been made. While all things share in this dream, as humans we share in this dream in a special manner. This is the entrancement, the magic of the world about us, its mystery, its ineffable quality."[45]

This magic of the world about us, the dream of the earth, is what activates our most profound human creativity. What's more, our most

---

*The quote in the previous note shows that this list ("perceiving, thinking," etc.) is what Thomas had in mind.

imaginative works of art "derive from the visionary power that is experienced most profoundly when we are immersed in the depths of our own being and of the cosmic order itself in the dreamworld that unfolds within us in our sleep, or in those visionary moments that seize upon us in our waking hours. There we discover the Platonic forms, the dreams of Brahman, the Hermetic mysteries, the divine ideas [discussed by] Thomas Aquinas, the infinite worlds of Giordano Bruno, the world soul of the Cambridge Platonists, the self-organizing universe of Ilya Prigogine, the archetypal world of C. G. Jung."[46]

The imaginable collective works of art that would constitute sustainable human cultures sometime in the future (like some cultures of the past) are those that would emerge from the dreamworld, cultures that would gradually take shape through the embodied visions of countless individuals. Such individuals, whom I call visionary artisans of cultural evolution, are the humans who each find a way to inscend—to "descen[d] into a more primitive state"[47]—and return with a piece of Brahmanic dream, Hermetic mystery, archetype, and so on, with which to build a never-before-seen component of an emerging sustainable culture.

Are the spontaneities within us, our instinctive resources, different from the guidance of the Earth and universe? Thomas said no, the spontaneities of both the Earth and the human derive from those of the universe: "The universe is so immediate to us, is such an intimate presence, that it escapes our notice, yet whatever authenticity exists in our cultural creations, is derived from these spontaneities within us, spontaneities that come from an abyss of energy and a capacity for intelligible order of which we have only the faintest glimmer in our conscious awareness."[48]

We might conclude, then, that "the spontaneities within us" are the ways we perceive, think, feel, imagine, speak, and act when we inhabit our authentic role in the world, the true place or niche for which nature designed us, individually and collectively, or as Thomas wrote, "our role in the planetary community." For me, *soul* is another word for this true place, role, or niche. ("Ultimate place" is the two-word definition of *soul* I suggest in *Nature and the Human Soul*.[49])

GENES, PLACE, SOUL, AND NATURE CODING

All of the above considerations form my basis for concluding that genetic coding, as biologists mean this phrase, is one aspect (the microbiological aspect) of how a DNA-based creature comes to exhibit the spontaneities that it does. But the spontaneities themselves are the primary phenomenon of interest when we speak about the way nature designed a living thing to be and act, while the phenomenon of genes is one part of Western science's explanation of how these spontaneities are passed from one generation to the next.

But genes are, in any case, only *one* part of this explanation. More generally, we might explain that our human spontaneities are what they are as a consequence of the *place* we have in Earth's ecology. We take the form we do and have the instincts and spontaneities we have because of the place we inhabit, our ecological niche. And, like every other member of the Earth community, our niche shifts and adjusts—or at least ought to—in relation to the activities of all other members of the Earth community. It's not simply or primarily about genes.

The idea that a thing is what it is by virtue of its relationship to all other things is at least as old as the Buddha's 500 BCE principle of dependent co-arising or interdependence and as modern as the notion, from general systems theory, of mutual causality.[50] As Thomas himself declared, "Nothing is itself without everything else."[51] And: "Each being of the planet is profoundly implicated in the existence and functioning of every other being of the planet."[52]

Place itself has a profound and primary effect on the nature of things. "Place" is not a mere description devoid of explanatory value. A thing is what it is and takes the shape that it does as a function of its place, role, or niche within its environment. A thing's place is the totality of relationships it has with all other things. Each environment is what it is by virtue of all the things in that environment and their relationships to one another.

How does our ecological place or niche determine our human form and spontaneities? Through relationship: our interactions with all the other creatures, plants, waters, air, and landforms. And these relationships gradually shift due to our behavior vis-à-vis all these others and theirs in relation to us. We adjust and adapt our behavior as a function of what we perceive, learn, need, value, and intend.

In recent decades, even the explanatory value of the gene has been significantly amended due to the intriguing wrinkle from the relatively new field of epigenetics: the expression or manifestation of a gene is now known to depend upon microbiological factors influenced by environmental and physiological events and processes. In other words, the effect a gene has on physiological form or behavior depends upon the presence and action of other elements in the environment. Everything is what it is by virtue of its relationship to everything else. Even the genetic manifestation of identical twins begins to diverge no later than birth.

I want to propose here that "genetic coding" is not the best way to identify what contrasts with our cultural coding; a clearer and more inclusive phrase, I believe, would be our "nature coding." By *nature coding* I refer to the ways in which our ecological niche (our place) and our own unconscious psyches influence our human form and tendencies. Our nature coding is how the Earth is dreaming us, even how the universe is doing so, independent of any conscious beliefs we have about ourselves.

Another way of referring to the influences of place and psyche, an alternative to *nature coding,* is *soul.* Our place, after all, is the soul's ecological manifestation, and psyche is the soul's psychological manifestation. Or said another way: Place or niche is how we experience the soul ecologically; numinous image or core identity (sense of our true self) is how we experience the soul psychologically.

Our genetic coding is part of how our nature coding operates, or one means by which our souls function.

With this concept of nature coding, I feel we can restate one of Thomas's central ideas, as follows: Our cultural coding, when healthy, derives from our nature coding. It's not that culture is unnatural, but that it's a second-order coding, one that we design (unlike our nature coding), and one that can diverge from our nature coding if we're not careful. Our nature coding is primary and foundational. Even our human ability to design our cultural coding is given to us by our nature coding. To become fully human, we require a healthy cultural coding in addition to our nature coding. But—and this is Thomas's point—if our cultural codings deviate from the guidance of our nature coding, then our cultures themselves become the greatest threat to our survival, as we are now witnessing throughout the world.

Cultural coding is necessary for humans to survive and mature, but not just any cultural coding will do. To keep our cultures vital, we must, in every generation, modify them by returning to their source in our nature coding. And when our cultures have entered a "destructive pathology," we must reinvent our cultures from the ground up by an even more extensive version of the same process. Thomas's word for this process of realigning culture with nature is *inscendence:* the descent to soul.

If we substitute the word *soul* or the phrase *nature coding* whenever Thomas wrote of "gene," "genetic endowment," or "genetic coding," we might obtain a more accurate and useful reading.

HUMAN DEVELOPMENT FROM
THE PERSPECTIVE OF INSCENDENCE

Human development is our most fundamental need in our current global mission: the Great Work of reinventing the human and relearning to embrace the dream of the Earth.

If reinventing the human depends upon inscendence, then human development must be a primary focus of our efforts at cultural transformation, for only developmentally mature individuals are able to experience inscendence and benefit from it. Inscendence is as psychospiritually challenging and risky as it is ecstatic and necessary for maturation beyond psychological adolescence.* Inscendence is the path to soul encounter. This encounter is what bestows the guiding vision for a lifetime, the mythopoetic template for personally belonging to the

---

Nature and the Human Soul describes the eight life stages of ecocentric/soulcentric human development. Soulcraft focuses specifically on the descent to soul, which is primarily associated with the fourth of the eight stages.

world in the way that the Earth and one's soul desire. Belonging to the world in this way is to contribute to the evolution and sustainability of one's culture—the sure sign of a true adult.

My estimate is that less than 20 percent of people in current Western and Westernized societies ever reach true adulthood.

Although human development is no more urgent a need than the infrastructural changes discussed earlier, it is our most *fundamental* need. The cultivation of authentic adulthood and genuine elderhood goes far beyond any modifications in how we generate energy or conduct business, agriculture, and politics. We need contemporary cultural codings that allow our full humanity to once again blossom. We need new, widely adopted practices for parenting children, educating them to become full members of not only a family and culture, but, equally important, of the Earth community as it exists in their particular bioregion. We require new, much more effective ways of supporting teenagers to uncover and embody their most authentic selves and, when ready, to learn the arts of inscendence so that they might explore the mysteries of nature and psyche and eventually, with good fortune, receive a vision revealing their unique place, role, or niche in the Earth community. By embodying this role, they become authentic adults, deeply imaginative artisans of cultural evolution.

We also need in each society a significant number of mature adults who have been called by the spontaneities within them to serve as guides to the initiatory rituals of inscendence.

And we need true elders, like Thomas Berry, to oversee all of these endeavors as we make our way into the very uncertain and enormously auspicious future.

Despite our dire times, Thomas was hopeful to the end about our prospects. He derived his hope from the story of the universe itself: "In the immense story of the universe, that so many of these dangerous moments have been navigated successfully is some indication that the universe is for us rather than against us. We need only summon these forces to our support in order to succeed. Although the human challenge to these purposes must never be underestimated, it is difficult to believe that the larger purposes of the universe or of the planet Earth will ultimately be thwarted."[53]

6

Dreaming in Sacred Sites

A Study and Tribute to Thomas Berry

Stanley Krippner, Paul Devereux,
Adam Fish, Robert Tartz, and Allan Combs

Thomas Berry described himself as an "Earth Scholar." Postmodernists would describe his worldview as one that conceptualized the universe as the only "text" for which there is no "context."[1] In other words, the evolving universe is primary and self-referential. But he also saw the universe as "story," and this story, for him, was the basic reality of human existence.[2] Berry sought ways to facilitate communication with other species, and even with the land itself, an exploration that leads toward activities that might save rather than despoil the Earth.[3,4] His focus was on the whole pattern of the Earth and its many communities. This broad vision is basic to many aspects of the postmodern agenda, including examples ranging from chaos and complexity theory to a growing appreciation of the worldviews of indigenous people.

Thomas described an "exceptional human experience," to use Rhea White's[5] term, that came to him at the age of twelve while he was walking in a meadow in the southeast United States.

It was an early afternoon in May when I first looked down over the scene and saw the meadow. The field was covered with lilies rising above the thick grass. A magic moment, this experience gave my life something. I know not what, that seems to explain my life at a more profound level than almost any other experience I can remember.

A more profound level at a more profound level than almost any other experience I can remember. It was not only the lilies. It was the singing of the crickets and the woodlands in the distance and the clouds in an otherwise clear sky. . . .

As the years pass, this moment returns to me, and whenever I think about my basic life attitude and the whole trend of my mind and the causes that I have given my efforts to, I seem to come back to this moment and the impact it has had on my feeling for what is real and worthwhile in life.[6]

For Berry, that field of lilies had become a "sacred site," one that existed in his memories more so than in physical reality. For indigenous people "sacred sites" are those geographical locations that a particular social group deems worthy of respect and veneration. Typically they are places of worship or used for other spiritual purposes. As such, they can be desecrated or defiled and hence are protected in one way or another. The ancient Greeks used the term *topos* to refer to the physical, observable features of a locale, and the word *chora* to refer to those qualities of a location that could trigger imagination and evoke a mythic presence.[7]

According to Vine Deloria Jr.,[8] a sacred site has the "ability to short-circuit logical process; it allows us to apprehend underlining unities." Rudolf Otto[9] used the term *numinous* to indicate the powerful experience of a holy place. According to some Native American traditions, one experiences these underlining unities through rituals held at such sacred places, or by entering these sites while in a changed state of consciousness. Those fortunate enough to have such experiences claim to sense a unification with nature, often including feelings of bliss as well as interspecies communication, waking visions, unusual sounds, synchronicities, and dramatic memories.[10] Another common theme is "the disappearance or transformation of familiar apprehensions of time and space."[11]

Deward Walker,[12] in describing the value of sacred sites, employed the concept "portal to the sacred." These portals are said to be trans-dimensional and cross-temporal "such that they become sacred times and spaces" to members of various cultural groups, even if those groups are separated in time. Carole Crumley[13] similarly observes that in many cultures, sacred places are considered liminal. Tucked between the mundane and spirit worlds, they are felt to be entry points into another consciousness.

This view of sacred places is well exemplified in the Hindu concept of the *tirtha*. The word derives from a Sanskrit verb meaning "to cross over," generally signifying a path or a passage. When applied to Hindu holy pilgrimage places (typically situated on rivers) it means "a crossing place." This is not only physically descriptive of many such sites but also deeply metaphorical.[14,15]

DREAMING AT SACRED SITES

Many Native American traditions attributed similar properties, such as encounters with spiritual agencies during nighttime dreaming,[16] to sacred sites. This was a conception shared by traditional cultures in Europe and other parts of the world. In commenting on these traditions, Paul Devereux has suggested treating prehistory as analogous to the human unconscious; "sacred places, it is suggested, may be those [that] yield greater information than secular ones; [they may be] locations where information is received more effectively by the unconscious mind."[17]

The designation of a site as sacred may result from its use as a crossing place or ford[18] or due to a discontinuity in the landscape, such as a sudden canyon, a shaft of white quartz, or a jagged peak.[19] Conversely, a sacred site might be the location of an alleged or actual spiritual event (a place where spiritual entities allegedly appeared, where a prophet was born or died, or where a sage's "enlightenment" or "awakening" took place). Another possibility is that the geophysical qualities of the location affected people's thoughts, feelings, or perceptions. Strabo (64 BCE–25 CE) wrote that the famed Oracle of Delphi breathed "vapor" from an opening in the earth before making her prophecies, an observation supported by recent archaeological research.[20] Traditional beliefs attributed these changed phenomenological states to occult powers, rather than to natural causes. For example, the Mescalero Apaches felt that a force known as *diya'* characterized intersections between the physical and spiritual worlds and that spiritual transformation could occur as people spent time in these locations.[21]

Transformation of one sort or another was sought through the practice of "temple sleep" in a place of worship or in a venerated natural site, with the aim of "incubating" dreams for initiation, divination, or healing. Ancient Jewish seers would spend the night in a grave or sepulchral vault, hoping that the spirit of the deceased would appear in a dream and offer information or guidance. Chinese incubation temples, where state officials would seek guidance, were active until the sixteenth century. In Japan the emperor had a dream hall in his palace where he would sleep on a polished stone bed when he needed assistance in resolving a matter of state. Dynastic Egypt had special temples for suppliants who would fast and recite prayers immediately before going to sleep. Before Thutmose IV (ca. 1419–1386 BCE) became ruler of Egypt, he related how the god Hormakhu appeared in a dream, foretelling of a united kingdom that would follow his ascension to power. When this came to pass, Thutmose IV recorded the dream on a pillar of stone that still stands before the Sphinx. Temple sleep was also popular in ancient Greece where more than three hundred dream temples were dedicated to Aesculapius, the god of healing.

The novelist and poet Lawrence Durrell made some astounding observations regarding his visit to two of these Greek dream temples.[22] In 1939 he made his first visit to one of the major Aesculapions, Epidaurus. He sensed that the whole area held an aura of sanctity— there was "something at once intimate and healing about it." But his Greek guide at the complex commented that he had managed to finagle a transfer to warden duty at Mycenae. Durrell wanted to know why the man should want to leave this green and peaceful place in favor of the craggy citadel. "I can't bear the dreams we have in this valley," the guide explained. "What dreams?" Durrell queried. "Everybody in this valley has dreams," the man replied. "Some people don't mind, but as for me, I'm off."

He went on to comment that the dreams frequently contained the figure of a man with an Assyrian-looking visage, with dense ringlets falling down onto his shoulders. He looked like a figure depicted in a fresco in the Epidaurus museum. It was an image of old Aesculapius himself, Durrell suspected. But surely that was to be expected, considering that the guide spent his days in Epidaurus? "Why should my two kids dream about him when they have never set foot in the museum?" the Greek retorted. "If you don't believe me, ask any of the peasants who live in this valley. They all have dreams. *The valley is full of dreams.*" Durrell wondered if the thousands of dreams countless suppliants had experienced at Epidaurus over its centuries of activity had somehow lingered on, or if it was some quality of the location.

In 1945, immediately after the Second World War, Durrell had reason to revisit this train of thought. While visiting the Greek island of Cos, he encountered two British soldiers who were clearing up scattered German and Italian ordnance; they were camped near the archaeologically excavated site of an Aesculapion. Durrell chatted with the soldiers who asked him if he knew anything about the temple. He told them about the Aesculapian cult and casually asked them if they had noticed anything unusual about their dreams. This startled them. It transpired that they had moved their tent out of their initial camping spot within the temple precinct precisely because they had experienced profoundly odd and disturbing dreams. "Was it possible, I found myself wondering again, that dreams do not disappear?" Durrell wrote. "And especially in a place like this which must have been charged with hundreds of thousands of dreams?"

Though the possible connection between sacred sites and dreaming has not been studied by Western science, there is a psychological literature regarding environmental influences on dreams. External stimuli may modify dream content, as when an externally administered spray of water is incorporated into a dream about a rainstorm, or cooling the feet by an external agent becomes associated with a dream of ice climbing in the polar regions. Examples such as these have been observed in sleep laboratories, while in a dreamer's ordinary surroundings the sound of a doorbell, for example, may evoke a dream in which a telephone is heard to be ringing.[23] With these ideas in mind the authors decided to investigate dreams reported by persons sleeping at sacred sites.

THE DRAGON PROJECT[24]

A customary observation in cosmologies throughout the world is that humans live on one dimension in a tiered cosmos. A transcendent vertical axis mundi connects the other dimensions and transects the ordinary world at special geographies.[25] Oftentimes, discontinuity in the landscape—a sudden canyon, a shaft of white quartz, a jagged spire—signals to the adept that an axis mundi is near. The Native Americans of the Columbia River Plateau in the inland Northwest felt that "points of geographic transitions are joined with multiple transitions" in seasonal, individual, and communal cycles. Thus, ecological transition zones and diurnal times—sunset and sunrise—are thought to be spiritually auspicious. Where these "points" transect are "especially powerful access points to the sacred."[26]

THE SITES

For this study, Paul Devereux, Dragon Project director, selected one site in Preseli, a hill range in Wales, and three sites in Cornwall, England. These were chosen on the basis of their prominence in local folklore as well as the practical fact that they afforded comfortable space for volunteers to sleep in sleeping bags or blankets during the night. The specific locations were Carn Ingli, Carn Euny, Chun Quoit, and Madron Well.

Carn Ingli ("Peak of Angels") is a jagged peak in the Preseli range of Wales, making it a prominent landmark. Preseli has been geologically identified as the source area for the "bluestones" of Stonehenge. Remnants of low, loose stone walls draped around the Carn Ingli peak may be evidence of veneration of the site in Neolithic or even Mesolithic times. In the sixth century, St. Brynach used the peak as a fasting and meditation retreat and claimed to have spoken with angels there. A local journalist learned of an incident in which a woman was thrown into an involuntary trance state on Carn Ingli and he reported it to the Dragon Project Trust. Its investigators subsequently detected full compass deflections on some of the rock surfaces, as well as in midair. Random checks at other peaks along the Preseli range did not produce similar findings.[27] There is some evidence that the megalith builders made specific use of magnetic stones in the construction of some of their monuments,[28] and such devices as Geiger counters have been utilized as investigative tools among archaeologists intrigued by possible radioactive and ultrasonic properties of the sites.[29]

Carn Euny is an Iron Age subterranean structure dating to roughly 500 BCE in the Land's End District of Cornwall. It consists of a stone passageway adjoining a corbelled beehive stone chamber. It is one of a class of structures archaeologically referred to as "souterrains" or, in Cornish dialect, *fogous*. Their function is unknown, and hypotheses have ranged from food storage to refuges to ritual chambers. The beehive chamber at Carn Euny is an unusual feature, though, and favors a ritual or ceremonial explanation. Because it is an enclosed structure made from blocks of granite, a naturally radioactive rock, its interior has higher levels of radiation than the outside base level. Archaeoacoustical research has also shown the chamber at Carn Euny to have a primary resonant frequency of 99 Hz, within the baritone range of the human voice.[30]

Chun Quoit, also in Land's End, Cornwall, is an isolated mushroom-shaped monument consisting of four inward-leaning slabs supporting a capstone and dates to ca. 3,000 BCE. It is of a monument type known as a "dolmen" and is located on a broad expanse of high moorland in exactly the right position for the midwinter sun to appear to set in a notch of the natural outcrop that stands prominently on the southwestern skyline. There have been reports of short bursts of light flashing across the underside of the capstone, and Geiger counter readings have detected high readings for radioactivity.[31] Again, archaeoacoustical research at this site has revealed a primary acoustical resonance of 110 Hz—well within the baritone range.[32] Recent neurophysiological research indicates that sound in the 95–125 Hz range can affect brain function in the frontal and temporal cortex.[33] This effect is most marked at 110 Hz.

Madron Well, likewise in Land's End, was once surrounded by massive blocks of granite (according to a 1910 photograph) and is located near the ruins of a medieval granite chapel. The footpath through the woods is a magical, green-hued walk suggestive of former times and beliefs. By the time the visitor reaches the turning for the well on the left, the twentieth century seems far away. Traditionally, this site has been associated with "feminine energy." Up until about the seventeenth century, a local "wisewoman" attended the actual spring. The spring water continues to be fed by stone conduit into a stone reservoir in the chapel's southwest corner.

Madron Well was celebrated for its purported healing properties and oracular powers, and part of the traditional healing procedure involved the patient sleeping within the chapel, one of the few documented cases of ostensibly Christian dream incubation in England. Presumably because it passes through granite conduits and is deposited into a granite reservoir, the water gives above-background radiation readings. In the 1600s a celebrated and documented case of healing took place here, when John Trelille allegedly became able-bodied after being crippled for sixteen years. He was bathed in the waters at the chapel once a week for three weeks, after which time he appeared to be fully healed and went on to live an active life as a soldier. The very essence of Celtic Christianity, with its powerful Pagan ancestry, seems to be here.

THE DREAMS

Several site dream reports contained descriptions or phrases reminiscent of ancient and mythical Cornwall, for example, "Jurassic rock," "a cave in the earth," "a stone tomb," "a labyrinth," "a stone circle," "a cave painting," "a hag," and "magicians." Nevertheless, the overall differences in dreams reported at the sacred sites compared to home dreaming were on the whole small and rather modest. Here it is perhaps well to remember a lesson learned the hard way over the years from parapsychological research. Dramatic events do occur and are reported by many people, but traditional scientific methods seem anathema to them, and only the most strenuous long-term investigations of this nature are likely to turn up significant results. In any event, allowing for a general sense to flow from this dream material, we may well have been glimpsing some site-associated resonances showing dimly through the distorting glass of personal dream recall.

CONCLUSION

The notion of sacred sites reflects a unity of human beings and their natural environment, a union that has been virtually forgotten in modern times but one that is well worth reestablishing.

The importance of rituals and beliefs that reflect the psychospiritual bond between humans and nature has been celebrated over the years by Thomas Berry.[34] Long before, as mentioned earlier, the Greeks developed two terms for place, *topos* and *chora*. (*Topos* signifies a simple location, the physical, observable features of a locale. *Chora*, however, refers to the more subtle aspects of place, those that can trigger memory, imagination, and mythic presence.) In the *Timaeus*, Plato claimed that chora could be known "in a kind of dream."[35] People who thought that they were in touch with chora as well as topos built sacred sites. One way to study a sacred site is to attempt to approximate the mind-frame of the builders and users of the site. In accordance with this notion, nighttime dreaming might put dreamers in touch with what David

Feinstein[36] refers to as the "mythic field" of these sites, the "stored" information of a "field" that may be accessed during altered states of consciousness.[37]

The wider implications of all this share the concerns of ecopsychology [38,39] as well as cognitive archaeology, a discipline that may result in healing the estrangement of Western scholars from their environment. Such perspectives offer a much needed antidote, because currently "wherever the Western mind goes, it marginalizes local, indigenous, and often, very different worldviews and systems of knowledge."[40] Visiting, studying, and spending time at sacred sites (as well as sleeping and dreaming there) can serve as reminders that one's state of consciousness and one's view of the land are inevitably tied to one another.[41]

7

The Double Life of Thomas Berry
Emergence and Evolution

—

Duane Elgin

The universe is a communion and a community.
We ourselves are that communion become conscious
of itself.

THOMAS BERRY

We bear the universe in our being
as the universe bears us in its being.
The two have a total presence to each other . . .

THOMAS BERRY

Thomas Berry was a deeply religious man who, I believe, would agree with the sentiments of William James who wrote in *The Varieties of Religious Experience,* "At bottom, the whole concern of religion is with the manner of our acceptance of the universe." Thomas both accepted and celebrated humanity's participation in the sacred story of an evolving universe. He is internationally known for his moving descriptions of the cosmos as it flowers over eons of time.

Without diminishing the importance of the "horizontal dimension" and the sacred nature of evolution, I want to appreciate another vector in the work of Thomas, and that is the "vertical dimension" or the

NOW, where the universe spontaneously emerges as a single system—a uni-verse. At every moment, rather than a collection of objects, we are, as Thomas so famously said, a "communion of subjects."

The power of Thomas's great work is that he recognizes we are living at the intersection of *both* evolution (unfolding ever greater diversity) *and* continuous creation (the entire universe is emerging as a unified whole at every moment). It is the doubly powerful nature of life at the intersection of emergence and evolution that gives such intensity and span of meaning to Thomas's dream for the Earth.

Looking at the life and writing of Thomas in this way, we can see two remarkable dynamics at work. The first is the "universe story" and is the grand narrative of the universe evolving over billions of years. The second dynamic is the "universe emerging" as a fresh creation at every moment. Where the universe story provides a stunning narrative of the "horizontal" unfolding *across* time, an emergent universe adds a further dimension—the "vertical" generation of the cosmos *in* time. The universe story focuses on the evolution of the universe *through* time and the emerging universe focuses on the universe being regenerated *in* time. The vertical dynamic of continuous creation slices through all that exists and reveals everything as a single orchestration happening all at once. We are, at every moment, a part of this grand unity of creation.

When the exquisite order and coherent unfolding of the universe *through time* combines with the extraordinary power of the universe emerging *in time* at an intersection called NOW, it reveals we simultaneously exist in a place of both creative freedom and profound communion. Being and becoming converge into an experience beyond words—and we recognize we already live in the realm of the sacred.

Our awakening to a new understanding of the universe in *both* its horizontal and its vertical aspect represents a stunning re-imagining of *where* we are and *who* we are as a species. Our awakening to the living universe goes beyond the history of any particular nation, region, or ethnic group. This vision of the human journey is big enough to honor the diversity of our past and to act as a beacon for our collective future.

This is a story of such immensity and immediacy that it completely transforms the shallow narrative of materialism and consumerism. The emerging narrative tears back the veil of presumed smallness and reveals humanity as creatures of cosmic dimension and participation. We are biocosmic beings who are awakening to life in an ever-emergent universe and an evolutionary task of developing ourselves in scope and subtlety, both personally and collectively.

Although the idea of an ever-emergent universe has ancient roots in human experience, it is also radically new and fresh as the frontiers of modern science are only now beginning to recognize how mysterious and magnificent the universe truly is. Humanity and the universe are becoming connected once again, but now with the aid of science to cut away superstition and reveal the authentic mystery and subtlety of our cosmic home.

Because our understanding of evolution is well-established (although still evolving), I want to focus on the other aspect in this powerful equation of existence—the continuous emergence of the universe as a unified system.

SCIENTIFIC VIEWS OF AN EMERGENT UNIVERSE

Is the idea of a continuously emerging universe supported by the sciences? From the frontiers of science, we are discovering that our universe has a number of key properties of emergent, living systems. I realize that some of these are controversial, and I refer the interested reader to my book *The Living Universe,* where they are explored in considerable detail.[1] Here I summarize six key attributes of our universe.

- *Completely Unified*—No longer is the universe regarded as a disconnected collection of planets, stars, and fragments of matter; instead, the powerful tools of science have demonstrated that "non-locality" exists. Even across vast distances, the universe is fully connected with itself. In the words of physicist, David Bohm, the universe is "an undivided wholeness in flowing movement."[2] This does not mean that scientists understand how this connectivity works—only that it is real and that, at a fundamental level, the universe is a fully unified system.

- *Mostly Invisible*—Scientists no longer think the visible stars and planets represent all there is in the universe. To their shock, they have recently discovered that the visible universe represents only 4 percent of the total universe—the other 96 percent is invisible. The invisible portion of the universe is comprised of two forces: one force is causing the universe to expand at an increasing rate (dark energy) and the other force is causing the universe to contract into clumps of stars and galaxies (dark matter).

- *Immense Background Energy*—Scientists used to think that empty space was essentially "empty." Now they realize there is an extraordinary amount of background energy permeating the universe, including empty space. Called "zero point energy," a cubic inch of seemingly empty space contains the equivalent of millions of atomic bombs worth of background energy.[3] We are swimming in an ocean of subtle energy of such immense power that it is incomprehensible in everyday human terms.

- *Continuously Regenerating*—The universe is not static, sitting quietly in empty space; instead, the totality of the universe is everywhere in motion and being regenerated moment by moment—a process requiring a stupendous amount of energy. This includes not only matter-energy but also the fabric of space-time. Despite the appearance of solidity and stability, the universe is a completely dynamic system. In the words of physicist Brian Swimme, "The universe emerges out of an all-nourishing abyss not only fourteen billion years ago but in every moment."[4] At every moment, the universe emerges as a single orchestration—a uni-verse or single verse of manifestation. Because nothing is left out of the regeneration of the universe, we are participants in a cosmic scale process whether we are conscious of it or not.

- *Consciousness at Every Scale*—An ancient and controversial idea is that we can find sentience or some form of consciousness at every level of the universe. Using sophisticated tools, scientists are now finding a spectrum of consciousness ranging from what might be called primary perception at the atomic and cellular level to a capacity for reflective consciousness at the human level.[5] From the atomic level to the human scale and in between, we find a capacity for reflection and choice that is fitting for that scale.

- *Freedom at the Foundations*—We do not live in a machine-like universe where everything is predictable. Instead, at the quantum foundations of existence, there is a buzzing world of probabilities and indeterminacy. Uncertainty and freedom are built in to the very foundations of material existence. We live in a world of probabilities, not certainties. Freedom and choice are real attributes of the universe and indicate the universe is a learning system.

When we bring these attributes together, we can then describe the universe as a unique kind of "living system." The universe is a unified and completely interdependent system that is continuously regenerated by the flow-through of phenomenal amounts of energy whose essential nature includes consciousness that supports some freedom of choice at every scale of existence. This transforms our understanding of the universe around us. We are immersed within the regenerative aliveness of an ever-emergent universe. The tools of science are suggesting the possibility that life and consciousness are *both* fundamental *and* emergent properties of the universe. In this view the cosmos is a single, living organism that is growing countless creatures within its embrace. This is not a new idea. More than two thousand years ago the Greek philosopher Plotinus described the universe as "a single living creature that encompasses all living creatures within it." This ancient insight is being explored again by modern science.

AN EMERGENT UNIVERSE IN WISDOM TRADITIONS

When we turn to the "inner sciences," what have sages across cultures and across the centuries discovered with regard to the universe? When men and women from diverse spiritual traditions invest years in deep meditation and contemplation, do they discover the universe to be a place of gray indifference without feeling qualities? Alternatively, does the universe reveal itself to us through the "spontaneities in our own being" as a place of ever-emerging mystery, vitality, and wholeness?

The understanding that we live in a living, regenerative universe is found in all of the world's major spiritual traditions. Christianity, Islam, Buddhism, Hinduism, indigenous traditions, and more, all speak to the idea of a regenerating universe. Here are a few, illustrative quotes:

> *God is creating the entire universe, fully and totally, in this present now. Everything God created . . . God creates now all at once.*
>
> MEISTER ECKHART,
> *MEDITATIONS WITH MEISTER ECKHART*

> *God keeps a firm hold on the heavens and earth, preventing them from vanishing away.*
>
> ISLAMIC KORAN, 35:41

> *Out of himself he brought forth the cosmos*
> *And entered into everything in it.*
> *There is nothing that does not come from him. . . .*
> *You are that . . . you are that.*
>
> HINDU, CHANDOGYA UPANISHAD

> *My solemn proclamation is that a new universe is created every moment.*
>
> D. T. SUZUKI, *ZEN AND JAPANESE CULTURE*

*The Tao is the sustaining Life-force and the mother of all
things; from it, all things rise and fall without cease.*

                    LAO-TZU, *TAO TE CHING*

*You have a death and a return in every moment. . . .
Every moment the world is renewed but we, in seeing
its continuity of appearance, are unaware of its being
renewed.*

                    RUMI, *THE ESSENTIAL RUMI*

*Evolution presupposes creation . . . creation is an ever-
lasting process—a* creatio continua.

                    POPE JOHN PAUL II

*At the heart of Buddhist cosmology is . . . the idea that
[multiple world systems, including our own universe] are
in a constant state of coming into being and passing away.*

                    DALAI LAMA, *THE UNIVERSE IN A SINGLE ATOM*

Based upon decades of research described in my book *The Living
Universe,* harvesting the wisdom of human experience is like watching a
picture gradually come into focus and seeing an extraordinary image of
the universe emerging before our eyes. Within each major tradition—
Christian, Muslim, Jewish, Hindu, Buddhist, Taoist, Confucian, indigenous, and more—we can find remarkably similar descriptions of the
universe and the life force that pervades it: *Christians* affirm that God
is not separate from this world but continuously creates it anew, so that
we live, move, and have our being in God. *Muslims* declare that the
entire universe is continually coming into being and that each moment
is a new "occasion" for Allah to create the universe. *Hindus* proclaim
that the entire universe is a single body that is being continually danced
into creation by a divine Life force, or Brahman. *Buddhists* state that
the entire universe arises freshly at every moment in an unceasing flow
of interdependent co-origination where everything depends upon every-

thing else. *Taoists* state that the Tao is the "Mother of the Universe," the inexhaustible source from which all things rise and fall without ceasing. *Confucians* view our universe as a unified and interpenetrating whole that is sustained and nourished by the vitality of the Life force, or *ch'i*. *Indigenous* peoples declare that an animating wind or Life force blows through all things in the world and there is aliveness and sacred power everywhere. A stream of *Western* thinkers portray the universe as a single, living creature that is continually regenerated and is evolving toward higher levels of complexity and consciousness. Overall, beneath the differences in language, a common reality is being described—our life is part of a larger life.

Despite our great diversity and differences of history, Thomas recognized that, when the world's wisdom traditions penetrate into the experiential depths of existence, a common understanding emerges about the universe that is in accord with insights from science. We live within a living universe that arises, moment-by-moment, as a unified whole. The universe is continuously sustained by the flow-through of phenomenal amounts of energy in an unutterably vast and intensely alive process of awesome precision and power. We are beings the universe inhabits as much as we are beings who inhabit the universe. The unity of existence is not an experience to be created; rather, it is an always-manifesting condition waiting to be appreciated and welcomed into awareness. The "power of now" derives from the fact that the entire universe arises in the NOW as an extremely precise flow. When we are in the now, we are riding the wave of continuous creation and each moment brings, seamlessly and flawlessly, a fresh formation of the entire universe.

LIVING AT THE CENTER OF THE CROSS

Thomas wrote of his experience of the generative aliveness of the universe with powerful conviction: "There is a certain triviality in any spiritual discipline that does not experience itself as supported by the spiritual as well as the physical dynamics of the entire cosmic-earth process."[6] He directly embodied the physical experience of sacred communion while speaking of the grand narrative of cosmic unfolding. It was clear from his heart-warming presence that these were interwoven realities for him—a singular experience in the moment. Thomas's dream was that we progressively awaken to the sacred context within which exists a living universe where we are a communion of co-learning subjects. Yet, he realized that humanity has barely begun to awaken to this great enterprise. The universe is so completely a part of ourselves, its subtle gifts escape our notice.

We are empowered when we become aware that the flow of our direct experience arises from the wisdom of creation that flows through and sustains the entire cosmos. He describes the intimate flow of the universe through us as experiencing the "spontaneities within our own being." "(W)hat we are ultimately groping toward, is the sensitivity required to understand and respond to the psychic energies deep in the very structure of reality itself."[7] This, he says, "is the ultimate lesson in physics, biology, and all the sciences, as it is the ultimate wisdom of tribal peoples and the fundamental teaching of the great civilizations."[8] We are "the psyche of the universe" but we are just beginning to consciously unfold this capacity.[9] Everyday life expresses "spontaneities that come from an abyss of energy and a capacity for intelligible order of which we have only the faintest glimmer in our conscious awareness." If the adage is true that "a potential recognized is a potential half-realized," then Thomas has given the world the enormous gift of recognizing (and beginning to realize) the "great work" that lies ahead for humanity.

In conclusion, I want to celebrate the double life of Thomas by acknowledging the two intersecting dimensions of his life and work—the horizontal and the vertical. In the horizontal dimension, he asks us to take the long view and feel compassion for the immensity of evolutionary development and learning that has brought us this far. In the vertical dimension, he asks us to connect intuitively with the structure of reality as a way for the universe to speak its wisdom through us. Thomas lived at the center of the cross where these two dimensions intersect one another, and the synergy of this intersection gives vitality and meaning to his dream for the Earth. Thomas's "dream" grows from a wide-awake vision that we live in a sacred universe—a living, learning system that is forever emerging as a unified whole while simultaneously growing ever more diverse expressions of its aliveness.

8

Ecological Interiority

Thomas Berry's
Integral Ecology Legacy

—

Sean Esbjörn-Hargens

What is needed, however, is the completion of the story of
the physical dimensions of the universe by an account of
the numinous and psychic dimensions of the universe.

THOMAS BERRY

I first encountered Thomas Berry's inspiring ecological vision as a graduate student by reading *The Dream of the Earth,*[1] *The Universe Story,*[2] and *The Great Work.*[3] Berry was an influential figure in my department: *Philosophy, Cosmology, and Consciousness* (PCC).* If anyone has had something meaningful to say about how these three realms of human inquiry and knowledge are interrelated it is Berry, with his articulation of the numinous cosmos and our "sacred Earth community." Under the academic tutelage of figures like Brian Swimme, Robert McDermott, Sean Kelly, Rick Tarnas, Mary Evelyn Tucker, and Charlene Spretnek, I made a deep study of the themes that are so prevalent in Berry's work.

---

*This department is housed within the California Institute of Integral Studies. I was there as a master's and then a doctoral student from 1999 to 2005.

Also, the inspiring eco-justice poet Drew Dellinger, whose acti*vision* has been deeply informed by Berry, was a fellow student. Hearing Drew perform on many occasions I was brought into direct contact with the embodied power of Berry's message. Thus, my academic training occurred in the rich loam soil of PCC with Berry's integral vision serving as one of the many suns fostering my own intellectual growth.*

This chapter is a celebration of Thomas Berry's ecological vision and an invitation for us to recognize the untapped potential of that vision for an integral approach to ecology. In particular this essay is a joy-filled observance of his emphasis on the interior dimensions of ecological and evolutionary realities.†

As a graduate student I devoted my academic studies to exploring and developing what I call *integral ecology*. I drew primarily on Ken Wilber's Integral Theory[4] and applied it to ecological science and environmental studies. I began using the term "integral ecology" in 1997 while serving as a Peace Corps volunteer and living in Chad, Africa. Now this was several years before becoming a graduate student and learning of Thomas Berry's integral eco-theology. Interestingly, years later Drew Dellinger told me that it was around 1995 that he recalls hearing Thomas Berry referring to his cosmological vision as an "integral cosmology or integral ecology."[5] So clearly, Berry himself used the term "integral ecology" also. In fact, in 2003 PCC had plans—which never really materialized—to launch the "Thomas Berry Institute for Integral Ecology," which was intended to offer a summer master's program in PCC with a focus on ecological thought and application. This impulse remained dormant for several years and resurfaced in 2007 in the form of an "integral ecology" track within the PCC curriculum.

In early 2005, I published a special double issue of Ervin Laszlo's

---

*In fact, my first-ever graduate level conference presentation occurred at "The Cosmological Imagination" conference in Berkeley, California (November 1–3, 2002), which was essentially a conference to pay tribute to Thomas Berry and included presenters such as Matthew Fox and Joanna Macy. The subject of my presentation was "Integral Ecology."
†Thanks go to fellow intefral ecologist Nick Hedlund for his comments and suggestions about an earlier revision of this essay.

journal *World Futures* on integral ecology with eight case studies.[6] In March of 2005, I defended my "integral ecology" dissertation and graduated.[7] I spent the next four years working with environmental philosopher Michael Zimmerman to transform my dissertation into an ambitious Wilberian presentation of integral ecology that accounts for more than two hundred distinct perspectives on the natural world.[8] What is interesting in this context is that while we mention Berry at a few places in our book (both praise and critique), Zimmerman and I do not draw on Berry to articulate our version of integral ecology.* Our effort is strictly a Wilberian one. This is noteworthy because Berry's integral corpus— spanning thirty years—is an amazing source of material for developing an alternative and complementary version of integral ecology. I say "integral corpus" because Berry often used the word "integral" in his discussion of the *New Story*. In fact, phrases like "integral vision," "integral ecological community," "integral functioning," and viewing humans as "integral members" of the Earth are found throughout his work.

Thus in this chapter I want to make a case for Thomas Berry's legacy as a pioneer of integral ecology—in particular a non-Wilberian integral ecology. I feel that we need multiple streams—overlapping and even contradictory ones—for integral ecology to flourish and mature. To this end I want to highlight one of the areas where I feel that Thomas Berry's vision can make a bold contribution to integral ecology and healing our planet. Namely, I want to explore his emphasis on the subjective dimension of organisms, or what I'm calling here *ecological interiority*. I am emphasizing the collective aspect of this interiority because Berry himself tended to talk about the ecological community and the

---

*For example, we note, "In 1988 Father Thomas Berry published his *The Dream of the Earth,* which clearly articulates an integrative approach to ecology. While he does not explicitly use the phrase 'integral ecology,' he uses the term 'integral' in a variety of ways throughout the book. Throughout this book, Berry discusses the evolution of consciousness, the development of cultures, the three value spheres of subjectivity, objectivity, and intersubjectivity. It is stunning the degree to which Berry foreshadows what we present here as integral ecology. We think the main difference between Berry's vision and ours is that integral theory provides a much more sophisticated framework for operationalizing his vision (which is no small task)" (Esbjörn-Hargens & Zimmerman, 2009a, pp. 541–42).

intimacy between beings that was needed to enter the Ecozoic Age.

This emphasis on ecological interiority overlaps with my own integral ecology commitments to integrate the interiority of organisms into ecological science. But Berry's vision brings his own unique style and emphasis to this important task. In doing this I want to both highlight one of many ways that Berry and Wilber share common ground, and I want to make a case that Berry has much to offer a non-Wilberian approach to integral ecology.* I hope this essay inspires others to explore his work, identifying ways in which it can contribute to the development of an integral ecology.

STREAMS OF INTEGRAL ECOLOGY

Before we explore one of Berry's contributions to integral ecology it will help to situate his voice within the landscape of integral ecological thinking. To my knowledge there have been at least four independent usages of the term *integral ecology*. The first usage of the term "integral ecology" appears to be in 1958 by Hilary Moore in a textbook on marine ecology. In the introduction he discusses the rift between the two major schools of ecology, those that focus on individual organisms or a single species (autecology) and those that study the entire ecosystem (synecology). He points out that "the protagonists of one [school of thought] sometimes fail to appreciate the true value of the other."[9] He goes on to suggest a third alternative: "The third facet is one that has so far been attempted only rarely but will certainly develop as our knowledge progresses: it might be termed integral ecology. The three parts form a circle, with synecology surveying the broad field, autecology differentiating this into its components, and integral ecology recombining these into the original whole."[10]

Cleary, Moore's impulse to name a third approach that could honor

---

*Additional areas of overlap between Berry's Universe Story and Wilber's Integral Theory include their embrace of evolution, human development, cultural development, nature as both harmonious and violent, the ultimate Mystery of reality, integrating science and religion, recognizing the psychic dimension of the universe, and embracing principles like: differentiation, subjectivity, and communion.

the truth of each of the other two schools is a harbinger of what will be needed as the field of ecology splits into even more camps than what existed in 1958.*

In 1995 Leonardo Boff, a liberation theologian living in Brazil, was editing (along with Virgil Elizondo) a special issue of *Concilium: The International Journal for Theology*. In the editorial that opens the issue, Boff and Elizondo called for an "integral ecology." After highlighting a variety of approaches to "ecological reflection," including conservationism, preservationism, environmentalism, human ecology, social ecology, and mental or deep ecology, they explain:

> The quest today is increasingly for an *integral ecology* that can articulate all these aspects with a view to founding a new alliance between societies and nature, which will result in the conservation of the patrimony of the earth, socio-cosmic well-being, and the maintenance of conditions that will allow evolution to continue on the course it has now been following for some fifteen thousand years.
>
> For an integral ecology, society and culture also belong to the ecological complex. Ecology is, then, the relationship that all bodies, animate and inanimate, natural and cultural, establish and maintain among themselves and with their surroundings. In this holistic perspective, economic, political, social, military, educational, urban, agricultural and other questions are all subject to ecological consideration. The basic question in ecology is this: to what extent do this or that science, technology, intuitional or personal activity, ideology or religion help either to support or to fracture the dynamic equilibrium that exists in the overall system.[11]

Also around this time, as noted above, we have Thomas Berry referring, at least informally, to his own work in this way. It is interesting

---

*In my study of the two hundred main perspectives on the natural world there are currently more than seventy schools of ecology (see the appendix in Esbjörn-Hargens and Zimmerman, 2009a). The field of ecology has exponentially exploded since the 1960s with the environmental movement, which developed right after Moore's text was published.

to note that given their shared Roman Catholic roots, Boff's liberation theology and its resulting integral ecology have much in common with Berry's eco-theology.* (More will be said about Berry's own version of integral ecology below.)

The fourth stream is the one based on Wilber's Integral Theory. It too is traced back to 1995 with the publication of *Sex, Ecology, Spirituality*[12]—a foundational text for the integral approach to the environment and the inspiration for my own coinage of "integral ecology" in 1997. In our book Zimmerman and I state:

Integral ecology recognizes levels of complexity in all four quadrants, or throughout all four perspectives: systems, behavior, experience, and culture:

- Ecosystems are comprised of and influenced by natural and social systems;
- Ecosystems involve the individual behaviors of organisms, at all scales (including microbes and humans). These organisms are understood as being members (not parts) of ecosystems;
- Members of ecosystems have various degrees of interiority (perception, experience, intentionality, and awareness); and
- Members of ecosystems interact within and across species to create horizons of shared meaning and understanding.[13]

---

*Not surprisingly, there is also a resonance between the vision that Boff and Elizondo offered and the one associated with Integral Theory. In fact, Boff's most systematic explication of his integral ecology occurs in his *Ecologia* published a few months before the editorial appeared in *Concilium* and later translated into English as *Cry of the Earth, Cry of the Poor* in 1997. For additional information on Boff's ecological approach to Liberation Theology, see his *Ecology and Liberation*. In spite of Boff's initial usage, the phrase "integral ecology" does not seem to occur in any other of his publications, though his work is clearly guided by an integral sensibility. This is most readily seen in his exposé of the limits of many contemporary approaches, his discussion of inner and outer ecologies, and his appreciation for Felix Guattari's *The Three Ecologies*. In spite of the compatibility that exists between Boff's vision and integral theory, there are some important differences. For example, Boff's approach has no model that accounts for personal, cultural, and social development. Also, Boff has a tendency to romanticize indigenous peoples, which is honorable given that he represents Catholicism, which has a long history of brutalization toward indigenous cultures. Nevertheless, integral theory suggests caution lest we fall into naive presentations and forms of cultural appropriation.

We go on later to provide a specific definition of integral ecology that builds on the classical one: the study of the interrelationship between organisms and their environment. The point is that we don't need a new definition of ecology per se to support a vision like Berry's. All we need to do is simply bring an integral view to this traditional formulation about organisms and their environments. By including the "psychic" dimension of all the members of the sacred Earth community, ecology becomes the study of the interrelationship between organisms' experiences and behaviors and their cultural and systems environments. Or as we state: "[*I*]*ntegral ecology is the study of the subjective and objective aspects of organisms in relationship to their intersubjective and interobjective environments at all levels of depth and complexity.*"[14] The difference here is that by "organism" we mean an individual being with subjectivity, and by "environment" we mean a community with intersubjectivity. Thus, an integral interpretation of the standard definitions of ecology recognizes organisms and their environments as having interiority.

As we will see, Berry has much to say about this kind of approach, which is why his voice as an integral ecologist is so important for all of us to register and amplify. To date, of these four integral ecology streams outlined above, the Wilberian one has been the most visible and well established.* There are also a number of other notable minor or related streams. However, I would hate for integral ecology to be dominated by a Wilberian orientation and in the process overshadow Berry's own contributions. So this essay is a clarion call for all of us to recognize Berry's legacy as a pioneer of integral ecology and to deepen our relationship to

---

*Other emerging integral ecology streams include Gilles Deleuze and Félix Guattari's geophilosophy (see Mickey 2010) and Edgar Morin's complex thought (see Kelly 2007; Esbjörn-Hargens & Zimmerman, 2009a, pp. 542–43). Both of these streams are quite promising and will add a lot to the current landscape of integral ecological thought. It is also worth mentioning the work of German philosopher Jochen Kirchhoff, who refers to his own position as "integral depth ecology" (*integrale Tiefenökologie*) (see Krüger, 2006). Kirchhoff's cosmological vision draws on Wilber's work to some degree, but it is not Wilberian. Also, the outdoor educator Michael Cohen (1993) has also used "integrated ecology" to describe his approach to wilderness therapy or nature counseling.

what he was pointing to so it can more fully inform our integral action in the world.

So it seems that in spite of Hilary Moore's early usage in the late '50s, it is 1995 that more accurately marks the birth of integral ecology. It was this year that Wilber's *Sex, Ecology, Spirituality*—a foundational text for an integral approach to the environment—was published.* In that same year the first published usage of the phrase "integral ecology" occurred via Boff and Elizondo. And during this period Thomas Berry, an important integral ecological writer and thinker, is known to have referred at times to his own work informally as "integral ecology." It is perhaps an indication that an idea's time has come when it appears in different contexts, each independent of the other. Perhaps this also serves as a reminder that such an approach need not be contained within any single framework or approach. One of the reasons I have taken time in the pages above to lay out Berry's implicit role in my graduate program and the various streams of integral ecology is to show how, to date, Berry's immense contribution has been under-served. By actively placing Berry next to figures like Wilber, Boff, Guattari, Morin, and others, we contribute to the task that Berry was so committed to in his life: a new story of the universe and our place in it.

With that I will now turn our attention to one of Berry's unique contributions toward an integral ecology: *ecological interiority*.

A COMMUNITY OF SUBJECTS

I want to turn now to what might be the most commonly quoted statement by Berry: "The universe is a communion of subjects, not a collection of objects."[15] If I had to summarize Berry's integral ecology, I

---

*Even Wilber does not explicitly use "integral ecology" in published material until five years later with the formation of the Integral Institute in 2000 and its resulting Integral Ecology Center (www.integralecologycenter.org) and the publication of *A Theory of Everything* (see pp. 97–99). Though some of his online postings did contain this phrase a year before this book was published.

would start here. Not just because it has become a mantra of sorts for many people but because it speaks directly to one of the things that Berry constantly is reminding us about: the Earth is comprised of *a community of subjects*. This lies at the heart of what I feel Berry has to offer—an integral ecology. One of the radical claims that integral ecology makes is that the web of life isn't just a complex network of exterior strands of energy flows and holistic inputs/outputs, but it is also at the same time a space of intimacy among various ecological beings. In other words, organisms are not just parts of an ecosystem; they are partners within an ecocommunity. They are not just strands in a big eco-web but are also members of an intersubjective space. Organisms are subjects—they have interiors, they have lifeworlds. By recognizing this psychic dimension of all beings we profoundly shift—along the lines of what Berry kept pointing to—how we are in relationship to the Earth community.

Marc Bekoff, the renowned ecologist who has done much trailblazing work on including animal interiors in our ecological story, pointed out the synergy between our approach and Berry's: "As I read [*Integral Ecology*] I often thought of Thomas Berry's claim that each and every individual is a member of a communion of subjects. The authors insist on returning "interiority" to the conversation about humankind and nature. Any ecological view that doesn't consider the depths and interconnections among all components of nature is only a 'partial ecology' rather than an 'integrated ecology' and misrepresents the magnificent webs of nature that abound all over the place."[16]

Bekoff goes on to say something else that clearly echoes Berry's own view of ecocommunity: "The science of ecology has excluded the interiors of ecosystem members for too long! The experiences and lives of animals and all sorts of vegetation are all bound into a social nexus and all members are indispensable for maintaining the integrated whole of nature. Let's not forget that vegetation can also have social lives. Suffice it to say, and to risk being trite, the deep reciprocal interconnections among members of the earth community are such that we're all in this together, and we all need others we can lean on."[17]

Now compare this last quote from Bekoff to Berry's own words in *The Dream of the Earth*: "If the demand for objectivity and the quantitative aspect of the real has led scientists to neglect subjectivity and the qualitative aspect of the real, this has been until now a condition for fulfilling their historical task. The most notable single development within science in recent years, however, has been a growing awareness of the integral physical-psychic dimension of reality."[18]

And now read this quote from Berry's essay "The Spirituality of the Earth": "The universe is not a vast smudge of matter, some jelly-like substance extended indefinitely in space. Nor is the universe a collection of unrelated particles. The universe is, rather, a vast multiplicity of individual realities with both qualitative and quantitative differences all in spiritual-physical communion with each other."[19]

Berry often talks about the numinous, psychic aspects of species and matter in the context of Earth as a sacred community. For Berry this is a crucial chapter in the new story, which is an integral story about Earth and its cosmic significance. He is very clear on the importance of recognizing ecological interiority: "Nothing on earth [is] a mere 'thing.' Every being [has] its own divine, numinous subjectivity, its self, its center, its unique identity. Every being [is] a presence to every other being."[20]

Berry, as many know, was deeply influenced by the Jesuit paleontologist Pierre Teilhard de Chardin (1881–1955). As Mary Evelyn Tucker notes of the many influences that Teilhard had on Berry one that stands out is his ". . . understanding of the psychic-physical character of the unfolding universe. . . . [and that] from the beginning some form of consciousness or interiority has been present in the process of evolution. . . . Consciousness, then is an intrinsic part of reality and is the thread that links all life-forms."[21]

As Berry observes, "While Darwin saw the human appearing only out of the physical earth, Teilhard de Chardin saw the human emerging out of both the physical and the psychic dimensions of the earth."[22] Berry was clear that Teilhard's view of the psychic-physical dimension of the universe from the very beginning was a key element that needed to be further developed and extended.[23] He eloquently explains: "There in the stars is where the primordial elements take shape in both their physical and psychic aspects. Out of these elements the solar system and the earth took shape, and out of the earth, ourselves."[24] So not only are we made of stardust but also that stardust is numinous with interiority.

Given the centrality of Teilhard's thought for Berry in general and in the context of ecological interiority, it is worth quoting Teilhard here. In his stunning chapter from *The Phenomenon of Man* titled "The Within of Things," Teilhard explains:

> It is impossible to deny that, deep within ourselves, an "interior" appears at the heart of beings, as it were seen through a rent. This is enough to ensure that, in one degree or another, this "interior" should obtrude itself as existing everywhere in nature from all time. Since the stuff of the universe has an inner aspect at one point of itself, there is necessarily a *double aspect to its structure,* that is to say in every region of space and time—in the same way, for instance, as it is granular: *co-extensive with their Without, there is a Within to things.*[25]

In a note linked to the paragraph that follows this, Teilhard clarifies: "Here, and throughout this book, the term 'consciousness' is taken in its widest sense to indicate every kind of psychicism, from the most rudimentary forms of interior perception imaginable to the human phenomenon of reflective thought."[26] Clearly this is in keeping with one of the most fundamental and radical tenets of integral ecology—with exterior ecosystems come interior ecocommunities. And there is no one more poetic in expressing this valuable and inspiring truth than Thomas Berry (I have chosen to quote him at length throughout this section of the essay—so that you can experience the direct inspiration that characterizes my own encounter with his provocative vision). Referring to himself at times as a *geologian,* he highlights the divine nature of an Earth that is comprised of exteriors and interiors: "That there is an organizing force within the earth process with both physical and psychic dimensions needs to be acknowledged in language and in imagery. It needs to be named and spoken of in its integral form. It has a unified functioning similar to the more particular organisms with which we are acquainted. When we speak of Earth we are speaking of a numinous maternal principle in and through which the total complex of Earth phenomena takes its shape."[27]

By way of concluding I want to reflect with you on some of the implications of Berry's view of ecological interiority for ecological theory and practice. The field of integral ecology can be an ecology fed by numerous streams of integral ecology, with Berry's own integral vision being an important confluence in that resulting meta-ecology.

CONCLUSION

Thomas Berry has gifted us with a powerful vision of what it means to be a member of the Earth community at the beginning of the Ecozoic Era, an era characterized as a ". . . period when human conduct will be guided by the ideal of an integral earth community, a period when humans will be present upon the Earth in a mutually enhancing manner."[28] Berry has provided us with many pointers as to how we might dream the Earth anew. It is up to us to allow his prophetic vision to inform our actions on behalf of a larger Earth community.

What would our world look like if we took seriously—in our laws, in our environmental assessments, in our ecological science—the reality of ecological interiority as articulated by Berry? How would it change business as usual? For example, Berry calls for an Earth jurisprudence and explains, "An interspecies jurisprudence is needed. The primary community is not the human community, it is the Earth community. Our primary obligations and allegiances are to this larger community."[29] This call is being headed and taken up by individual lawyers and university law programs.* More legal and policy work needs to be done that takes the psychic dimension of our Earth community members seriously, but this is a great start.

In addition to Marc Bekoff's important work[30] as an ecologist,

---

*For more information on Earth jurisprudence, see the Center for Earth Jurisprudence at www.earthjuris.org.

including that on interiors, there are additional examples of trained ecologists incorporating the value of animal interiority in their fieldwork. For example, Joel Berger's analysis of the role that fear plays in predator-prey relationships is revealing a lot about culturally transmitted emotions with social animals such as moose and elk.[31] There is also the stunning work of G. A. Bradshaw, who has a doctorate in both ecology and psychology.[32] She has studied the minds and cultures of elephants and shed light on how trauma (e.g., a calf witnessing its parents being killed by poachers) is experienced and how it manifests in ecological behaviors. These are just two examples, but they point in the direction of the value of Berry's view of ecological interiority and how such a view can be married with the more mainstream scientific approaches, thereby achieving what Berry's lifework calls for—an integral story: a story that includes both the exteriors and the interiors of all expressions of the cosmos.

May we continue to be inspired by Berry's own deep intimacy with the cosmos wherein he resonated with the shared depth of all matter. May we embrace the integral ecology legacy that Berry has left us with and continue to engage his cosmological sensitivities to foster a sacred Earth community wherein the interiority of all members is recognized and celebrated. In this spirit, I leave you with an excerpt from Drew Dellinger's poem "Carolina Prophet: Poem for Thomas Berry."[33]

> *white hair communing with angels of Earth*
>
> *Father Thomas, reminding us*
> *we are constantly bathed in shimmering memories*
> *of originating radiance*
>
> *we are constantly bathed in shimmering memories*
> *of originating radiance*
>
> *the psychic stars:*
> *the conscious soil.*

9

Earth Community

What It Tells Us about Faith and Power

❦

Joanna Macy

No concept put forth by Thomas Berry appears more compelling for this historical moment than that of Earth community. It represents, as he says, the transformation of our worldview from "an anthropocentric norm and value to a biocentric or geocentric norm." Because industrial society is unable to deal with the ecological crisis it has induced, Berry argues that nothing less than the recognition of the Earth as "our primary community" can ensure the survival of complex life-forms. This necessary shift in perception, he affirms, "will affect every aspect of our human thought and action. It will affect language, religion, morality, economics, education, science, technology, and medicine." On a deeper level, it promises to bring quite different understandings of the meaning of faith and the nature of power.

The words Earth community take me back to a morning in Great Britain. I was standing for an hour in the sweet, gentle, English drizzle. With me in a large meadow were about forty men and women; three of them held toddlers. We stood in a circle and in the center rose two ancient, sacred stones. We had come there at the close of a five-day workshop on ecology, and our band included activists from every region of the Emerald Isle—social workers, civil servants, artisans, teachers, homemakers—drawn together by a common concern for the fate of our planet.

In the presence of the standing stones, thousands of years old, we seemed to find ourselves in two dimensions of time simultaneously. One was vast and immeasurable. As we reached back to the ancient Earth wisdom of the culture that erected the stones, we sensed the long, long journey of life unfolding on this planet. At the same time, we were acutely aware of this particular historical moment, when forces that our culture has unleashed, are on the way to destroying our world.

Among us were Christians, Jews, Buddhists, and Pagans. Yet, despite the differing traditions to which we belonged, the prayers and affirmations that spontaneously arose in that circle expressed a common faith and fueled a common hope. Those words bespoke a shared commitment to engage in actions and changes in lifestyle on behalf of our Earth and its beings. They expressed a bonding to this Earth, going beyond feeling sorry for the planet or feeling scared for ourselves. They were an affirmation of relationship—relationship that can be spiritually as well as physically sustaining, a relationship that can empower.

Faith is an elusive and questionable commodity in these days of a dying culture. Where do you find it? If you've lost a faith, can you invent one? Which faith to choose? Some of us have retained a faith in a just creator God or in a lawful, benevolent order to the universe. But some of us find it hard, even obscene, to believe in an abiding providence in a world of such absurdity that, in the face of unimaginable suffering, most of our wealth and wits are devoted to making profits and war. For a final holocaust we hardly need bombs; it is going on right now in the demolition of the great rain forests and the poisoning of our seas, soil, and air.

In a world like this, what can faith mean? The very notion can appear distasteful when we see faith used as an excuse for denial and inaction. "God won't let it happen." Or even, in some circles today, "It is God's will," a fearful assertion indeed when it refers to some final and holy battle to exterminate the wicked. The radical uncertainties of our time breed distortions of faith, where fundamentalist beliefs foster self-righteousness and deep divisions that turn patriotism into xenophobia, breeding hatred of dissent and feeding the engines of war.

Another option opens, however, that can lead to a more profound and authentic form of faith. We can turn from the search for personal salvation or some hypothetical haven, and look instead to our actual experience. When we simply attend to what we see, feel, and know is happening to our world, we find authenticity. Going down into a darkness where despair lurks and comforts dissolve, we can make three important discoveries.

I see them as redeeming discoveries that can ground us in community and serve as our faith. These three are: (1) the discovery of what we know and feel, (2) the discovery of what we are, and (3) the discovery of what can happen through us—or, one could say, grace.

DISCOVERING WHAT WE KNOW AND FEEL

To discover what we know and feel is not as easy as it sounds. In contemporary industrial society a great deal of effort and expense is devoted to keeping us from that raw honesty. Entire industries are focused on persuading us that we are happy, or on the verge of being happy, as soon as we buy this toothpaste or that automobile. It is not in the perceived self-interest of multinational corporations, or the government and the media that serve them, that we stop and become aware of our anguish with the way things are.

This de facto censorship or taboo is quite an accomplishment since none of us, in our hearts, is free of sorrow for the suffering of other beings. None of us is indifferent to the dangers that threaten our planet, or unburdened by fear for the generations to come. Yet it is not easy to give credence to this anguish in a culture that still enjoins us to "keep smiling" and "go shopping."

No dangers we face are as great as the blocking of our natural responses to them; it deadens both the mind and the heart. Robert Jay Lifton, the psychiatrist who pioneered the study of the psychological effects of nuclear bombing, points out that the refusal to acknowledge these responses, or even feel them, leads to psychic numbing. It divorces our mental calculations from our intuitive, emotional, and biological embeddedness in the matrix of life. It leads to a profound and dangerous splitting that allows us to acquiesce in preparations for our own demise.

As argued by sociologist Joel Kovel, author of *The Enemy of Nature: The End of Capitalism or the End of the World,* we are made subservient and passive by "the state of nuclear terror." This terror is not fear of weapons of mass annihilation so much as our fear of that fear. We are afraid that we might break apart or get stuck in despair if we were really to open our eyes. So the messages we tend to hear and to give are: "Don't talk to me about acid rain, or the arms race. There is nothing I can do about it. I have a family to support, a job to keep. If I were to take it all in and allow myself to think or feel it, I wouldn't be able to function."

So the first discovery, that of opening to what we know and feel, takes courage. Like Gandhi's *satyagraha,* it involves "truth-force." People are not going to find their truth-force or inner authority in listening to the military or industrial "experts," but in listening to themselves. Every one of us is an expert on what it is like to live on an endangered planet.

To affirm that shared awareness, and counter habits of repression, a form of group work known as the *Work That Reconnects* has evolved over the past thirty years. Its theory and methodology, drawn from deep ecology, systems theory, and Buddhist teachings, bring people together to find their own inner authority. Without mincing words, without apology, embarrassment, or fear of causing distress, they simply tell the truth of what they see and sense is happening to their world. A boy speaks of the dead and dying fish in a stream he loves; young parents express their dread of Strontium 90 in their children's bones. To quote Justin Kenrick, a colleague in this work:

We need permission in our minds and hearts and guts to accept that we are destroying the Earth and to feel the reality of who we are in that context; isolated, desperate, and powerless individuals, defeated by our old patterns of behavior before we have even begun to try to heal our lives and the Earth. Only then can we give ourselves permission to feel the power our culture denies us, to regain our intuitive sense of everything being in relation rather than in opposition, to regain our intuitive sense of the deep miraculous pattern to life that opens to us as we accept it.

In acknowledging our pain for the world, we return to the literal meaning of *compassion:* "to suffer with." Suffering with our world, we are drawn into the cauldron of compassion. And as Kenrick's words suggest, it reconnects us with each other and with our power.

DISCOVERING WHAT WE ARE

Acknowledging the depths and reaches of our inner responses to the demise of our world, we come to the second discovery: the discovery of *what* we are. The pain we feel for our world is living proof of our mutual belonging. Our raw capacity to "suffer with" testifies to an innate wellspring of compassion. This natural endowment is seen in Mahayana Buddhism as the mark of the *bodhisattva*. The tradition's model for heroic behavior, the bodhisattva is also, by virtue of our interexistence in the web of life, each person's true nature. Knowing that there is no such thing as private salvation, nor healing without contact, he or she does not try to escape from this suffering world or hold aloof from its pain.

The scriptures tell us that we are all bodhisattvas, and our radical interconnectedness is portrayed in the beautiful image of the Jeweled Net of Indra. It is similar to the holographic model of the universe we find emerging from contemporary science. In the cosmic canopy of Indra's Net each of us is a multifaceted jewel at each node of the net. Every jewel reflects all the others and sees the others reflecting back.

That is what we find when we hear the sounds of the Earth crying within us. The tears that come are not ours alone; they are the tears of an Iraqi mother looking for her children in the rubble; they are the tears of a Navajo uranium miner learning that he is dying of cancer. We find we are interwoven threads in the intricate tapestry of life, its deep ecology, its Earth community.

What happens for us then is what every major religion has sought to offer—a shift in our sense of identity, a turning from the isolated, ego-centered "I" to a vaster sense of what we are. This is not only a spiritual experience but also an evolutionary development understandable in systems cybernetic terms. As living forms evolve on this planet, they move not only in the direction of diversification but also toward integration as well. These two movements complement and enhance each other. Open systems self-organize and integrate by virtue of their differentiation, and they differentiate by virtue of their interactions.

In our evolution as life-forms, we progressively shed our shells, our armor, our separate encasements. We grew sensitive and vulnerable protuberances—eyes, lips, fingertips—the better to connect and receive information, the better to interweave our discoveries. If we are all bodhisattvas, it is because of that natural, inalienable thrust to connect, that capacity to integrate with and through each other.

In his book *Ecology and Man,* Paul Shepard writes: "We are hidden from ourselves by patterns of perception. Our thought forms, our language, encourage us to see ourselves or a plant or an animal as an isolated sac, a thing, a contained self, whereas the epidermis of the skin is ecologically like a pond surface or a forest soil, not a shell so much as a delicate interpenetration." Paul Shepard is calling us to a faith in our very biology. He goes on to say, "Affirmation of its own organic essence will be the ultimate test of the human mind."

We begin to see that a shift of identification can release us not only from the prison cell of ego but also from the tight compartment of a solely human perspective. As John Seed, founder of the Rainforest Information Center in Australia, points out, it takes us "beyond anthropocentrism." In his essay by that title, he says that anthropocentrism or human chauvinism is similar to sexism, but substitute "human race" for man and "all other species" for woman. And he says:

> When humans investigate and see through their layers of anthropocentric self-cherishing, a most profound change in consciousness begins to take place. Alienation subsides. The human is no longer an outsider apart. Your humanness is then recognized as being merely the most recent stage of your existence; as you stop identifying exclusively with this chapter, you start to get in touch with yourself as vertebrate, as mammal, as species only recently emerged from the rainforest. As the fog of amnesia disperses, there is a transformation in your relationship to other species and in your commitment to them. . . . The thousands of years of imagined separation are over and we can begin to recall our true nature; that is, the change is a spiritual one—thinking like a mountain, sometimes referred to as deep ecology. As your memory improves . . . there is an identification with all life. . . . Remember our childhood as rocks, as lava? Rocks contain the potentiality to weave themselves into such stuff as this. We are the rocks dancing.

BEING ACTED THROUGH

That leads us to a third discovery we make in the arising of Earth community. It is the discovery of what can happen *through* us. If we are the rocks dancing, then that which evolved us from those rocks carries us forward now and sustains us in our work for the continuance of life.

When I admired a nurse for her strength and devotion in keeping long hours in the children's ward, she shrugged off my compliment as if it were entirely misplaced. "It's not *my* strength, you know. I get it from the life in *them*," she said, nodding at the rows of cots and cribs. "They give me what I need to keep going." Whether tending a garden or cooking in a soup kitchen, there is the sense of being sustained by something beyond one's own individual power, of being acted *through*. It is close to the religious concept of grace, but distinct from the traditional Western understanding of grace, as it does not require belief in God or a supernatural agency. One simply finds oneself empowered to act on behalf of other beings—or on behalf of the larger whole—and the empowerment itself seems to come *through* that or those for whose sake one acts. In the systems view, this phenomenon can be understood as synergy. It helps us recast the very notion of what power is.

Since, as Berry makes clear, it is constituted of relations between subjects, rather than subjects and objects, our Earth community is, by its nature, self-organizing. The open systems that comprise it—be they cells or organisms, cedars or swamps—require no external or superior agency to regulate them, any more than your liver or an apple tree needs to be told how to function. In other words, order is implicit in life; mind is not separate from nature but integral to life processes. This, of course, contrasts with the hierarchical worldview our mainstream culture held for centuries, where mind is set above nature and where order is assumed to be something imposed from above on otherwise random, material stuff. We have tended to define power in the same way, seeing it as imposed from above. We have equated power with domination, with one thing exerting its will over another. It becomes a zero-sum or win-lose game, where to be powerful means to resist the influences and reduce the options of the other, and where strong defenses are necessary to maintain one's advantage.

In falling into this way of thinking, we lost sight of the fact that this is not the way nature works. Living systems evolve in complexity, flexibility, and intelligence through interaction with each other. These interactions require openness and vulnerability in order to process the flow-through of energy and information. They bring into play new responses and new possibilities, increasing the capacity to effect change. This interdependent release of fresh potential, this synergy, is like grace because it brings an increase of power beyond one's own capacity or private resources.

THE POWER TO CONNECT

Aroused by the very dangers we face, this kind of grace is happening right now and on a planetary scale; I see it everywhere I go. I see it in grassroots' responses to the climate crisis in virtually every country. During the late 2009 Copenhagen climate summit, local demonstrations for a greenhouse gas limit of 350 parts per million amounted to the largest public action in human history.

I see it in the proliferation of farmers markets, urban gardens, permaculture projects, "edible schoolyards," and CSA (community-supported-agriculture) farms that are springing up as people act to ensure healthy, locally grown food and free themselves from agro-industry; and I see it as well in their global counterpart, the Via Campesina, the movement of peasant farmers resisting corporate takeovers of their land and markets. I see it in the rapid spread of local projects for clean energy, green jobs, and community banking and currencies. There are countless such innovative grassroots actions; they do not make headlines, but taken all together they amount to an unprecedented explosion of people who are quietly putting concern for our common fate ahead of personal profit or pleasure. They manifest what can happen *through* us when we break free of the old hierarchical notions of power. They show that grace happens when we act with others on behalf of our world.

Paul Hawken, in his carefully documented book, *Blessed Unrest,* estimates that such local efforts on the global scene have already spawned nongovernmental organizations numbering in the millions. He concludes that they constitute the largest social movement in history.

> It claims . . . no special powers and arises in small discrete ways, like blades of grass after a rain. This movement grows and spreads in every city and country, and involves virtually every tribe, culture, language, and religion, from Mongolians to Uzbets to Tamils. It is comprised on families in India, students in Australia, farmers in France, the landless in Brazil, the Bananeras of Honduras, the "poors" of Durban, villagers in Irian Jaya, indigenous tribes of Bolivia, and

housewives in Japan. . . . The quickening of the movement in recent years has come about through information technologies becoming increasingly accessible and affordable. Its clout resides in its ideas, not in force.

This immense arising of decentralized, interconnected human effort and ingenuity can be recognized as the transition from the industrial growth society to a life-sustaining civilization. The Great Turning is one name for this necessary revolution. Seeing its significance on an historical scale of millennia, economist David Korten calls it the Great Turning "from empire to Earth Community."

For the scientists and activists who see it most clearly, the accelerating destruction of the natural world offers little room for hope in a positive future. But in lieu of hope, if we know where to look, we can see synergy. Its novel and ingenious forms emerge like green shoots through the rubble of a dysfunctional civilization. They are easier to see when we've dared to trust our deep belonging to this broken world and when our eyes are washed by tears. Our inseparability—from each other and from the fragile, miraculous web of life—is the ground of both our faith and our power to act. Our sheer presence evokes that faith, and opens us to the power of Earth community as it awakens in us now.

Thomas Berry would have us believe in our right to be here and in the distinctive role we each can play in this awakening. "Every part of the universe activates a particular dimension or aspect of the universe in a unique and unrepeatable manner. Without the perfection of each part, something is lacking from the whole. Each particular being in the universe is needed by the entire universe. With this understanding of our profound kinship with all life, we can establish the basis for a flourishing Earth community."

10

Berry and the Shift from the Anthropocentric to the Ecological Age

Ervin Laszlo

In his essay "The Ecological Age," Thomas Berry wrote, "Presently we are entering another historical period, one that might be designated as the ecological age. I use the term *ecological* in its primary meaning as the relation of an organism to its environment, but also as an indication of the interdependence of all the living and nonliving systems of the earth." Entering this age is "not simply adaptation to a reduced supply of fuels or to some modification in our systems of social or economic controls. Nor is it some slight change in our educational system. What is happening is something of a far greater magnitude. It is a radical change in our mode of consciousness."[1]

We are on the threshold of a new age, and entering it calls for changing our mode of consciousness: this is the gist of Berry's message. Remarkably, he grasped both the enormity of the problem and the nature of its solution at a time when few others had recognized either the one or the other. Today we are discovering the truth of Berry's assessment. We begin to speak of a thorough transformation of the entire tenor of life on the planet—a "worldshift." And we are becoming aware that the way to accomplish it is not by throwing money and technology at the problems we face, but by changing the way we think of ourselves, of our environment, and of our relationship with the whole biosphere.

The challenge of transformation to the ecological age is a challenge to our mode of consciousness—and because our consciousness is what primarily determines our values, beliefs, and aims, it is a challenge to our entire mode of being. We are no longer "in sync" with the universe. Berry noted, "Our secular, rational, industrial society, with its amazing scientific insight and technological skills, has established the first radically anthropocentric society and has thereby broken the primary law of the universe, the law of the integrity of the universe, the law that every component member of the universe should be integral with every other member of the universe and that the primary norm of reality and value is the universe community itself in its various forms of expression, especially as realized on the planet Earth."[2]

The magnitude of the shift we face is not to be underestimated. It is local and global, economic and ecological, political as well as cultural. It involves our relationship with ourselves, with others, with nature, and with the cosmos. Its dimensions have been prophetically assessed by Thomas Berry. Here I shall merely provide some underpinning for his insight by pointing in concrete terms to the kind of beliefs and myths that dominate the current anthropocentric age, in order to contrast these beliefs and myths with the consciousness that would enable the human community to shift to the ecological age.[3]

THE DOMINANT BELIEFS AND MYTHS
OF THE ANTHROPOCENTRIC AGE—
AND WHY THEY ARE OBSOLETE

In our dealings with others, the bottom line is, "What do I get out of it?" The rest is icing on the cake, without real value and interest.

Getting is not the supreme value it is believed to be. We are social beings, and *giving* gives us pleasure, whether we admit it or not. Without the experienced value of giving there would not be a solid basis for community life. People who only want to get all that they can from others cannot make a functioning community. The value of giving is present in traditional societies. As anthropologists have found, for many Native Americans "the rich" are those who give to the community—not those who just see how much they can get for themselves.

We are separate individuals enclosed by our skin and pursuing our own interests. We have only ourselves to rely on; everyone else is either friend or foe, at best linked to us by temporarily coinciding interests.

That we are unique is true, but it doesn't mean that we are separate from each other and from nature. Seeing ourselves as separate from the world fuels selfish and irresponsible tendencies: we are only responsible for ourselves, and not for "foreigners," "competitors," and "others."

The problems we experience are but interludes after which everything goes back to normal. Business as unusual has evolved out of business as usual, and sooner or later reverses back into it.

If we remain convinced that the problems we encounter are but interludes in an unchanging and perhaps unchangeable status quo, no experience of the problems will change our thinking, and we shall continue to act as we always have, using at the most the "tried and tested" methods of coping—which could be totally inadequate in the new circumstances.

Order in society can only be achieved by rules and laws and their enforcement, and this requires a chain of command that is recognized and obeyed by all. A few people on top make the rules, legislate the laws, give the orders, and ensure compliance with them. Everyone else is to follow the rules and take his or her place in the social and political order.

Hierarchy is not a sound basis for order in society. Male-dominated hierarchies do not work well even in the army and the church, much less in business and society. Successful business managers have learned the advantages of lean structures and teamwork, but for the most part, social and political institutions still operate in the hierarchical mode, which makes their workings cumbersome and inefficient.

Whatever the problem, technology is the answer.

Technology is a powerful and sophisticated instrument, but it is only an instrument: its utility depends on how (and even on whether) it is used. Even the best technology is a two-edged sword. Nuclear reactors produce an almost unlimited supply of energy, but their waste products and their decommissioning pose still unsolved problems. Genetic engineering can create virus-resistant and protein-rich plants, improved breeds of animals, vast supplies of animal proteins, and microorganisms capable of producing proteins and hormones and improving photosynthesis, but it can also produce lethal biological weapons and pathogenic microorganisms and destroy the diversity and the balance of nature.

The newer is always better.

Current experience shows that this is not the case. Sometimes the new is worse than what it replaced—more expensive, less enduring, more complex and less manageable, and more damaging to our health and our environment. And the old may be not simply decrepit and outdated but could incorporate values and traditions that we would do well to remember and to preserve.

We owe allegiance only to one nation, one flag, and one government.

The chauvinistic slogan "my country, right or wrong" asks people to fight for causes their government espouses and may later repudiate and to embrace the values and worldviews of a small group of political leaders. It ignores the interdependence and the shared future of all people on the globe. There is nothing in the normal human mind that forbids the expansion of our loyalty above the level of our country. We can be loyal to our community without giving up loyalty to our province, state, or region. We can be loyal to our region and feel at one with an entire culture, and even with the human family as a whole.

There is a direct link between having money and being happy. The more money I have, the happier I am.

The belief about the link between wealth and happiness is not borne out by experience. Money can buy many things but not happiness and well-being. It can buy sex but not love, attention but not caring, information but not wisdom. Since 1957 the GNP in the United States has more than doubled, but the average level of happiness has declined: those who report being "very happy" are only 32 percent of the population. At the same time the divorce rate doubled, the teen suicide rate more than doubled, violent crime tripled, and more people than ever say they are depressed. We have big houses and broken homes, high income and low morale, secured rights and diminished civility.

Why should we worry about the welfare of the next generation? Every generation has always had to look after itself, and the next generation will have to do the same. The future is not our business.

Living without conscious forward planning—although it may have been sufficient in days of rapid and seemingly unlimited growth when every new generation appeared able to take care of itself—is not a responsible option at a time when what we think and how we act has profound implications for the well-being, and even the survival, of the generations that come after us.

The earth is an infinite source of resources and an infinite sink of wastes. For all intents and purposes, nature is inexhaustible.

The roots of this "Neolithic myth" reach back thousands of years. It would hardly have occurred to the inhabitants of ancient Babylonia, Sumer, Egypt, India, or China that the environment around them could ever be exhausted of the basic necessities of life—edible plants, domestic animals, clean water, and breathable air—or fouled by dumping waste and garbage. The environment appeared far too vast to be affected by what humans did in their settlements and on the lands that surround them.

In the course of the centuries, belief in the inexhaustibility of nature produced increasingly negative consequences. The Fertile Crescent of biblical times turned into the Middle East of today: a region with vast areas of arid and infertile land. In earlier days people could colonize virgin lands and exploit untapped resources. Today there are no more virgin lands, and aside from the sun, few if any major unused resources. In a globally extended industrial civilization wielding powerful technologies, the "Neolithic Illusion" is a dangerous myth. It gives free rein to the overuse of the planet's resources and disregards the limits of its regenerative capacities.

Nature is a giant mechanism that we can engineer to fit our needs and demands.

The myth that nature is a giant mechanism that can be engineered as we like stems from the early modern age; it is a carryover from the Newtonian view of the world. This myth was adapted to creating and operating medieval technologies—water mills and windmills, pumps, mechanical clocks, and animal-drawn plows and carriages—but it fails when it comes to interacting with the environment on a massive scale, with powerful technologies. The outcome is a plethora of "side effects," such as the degradation of water, air, and soil, the alteration of the climate, and the impairment of local and continental ecosystems.

Life is a struggle where the fittest survive and where the unfit are eliminated by competition, the societal equivalent of natural selection.

The "survival of the fittest" myth dates from the nineteenth century, a consequence of the transfer of Darwin's theory of evolution to the sphere of society. It is a tragic mistake. Already over a hundred years ago the English biologist Thomas Huxley pointed out that truly moral conduct—*goodness* or *virtue*—"involves a course of conduct that, in all respects, is opposed to that which leads to success in the cosmic struggle for existence. In place of ruthless self-assertion it demands self-restraint; in place of thrusting aside, or treading down, all competitors, it requires that the individual shall not merely respect, but shall help his fellows; its influence is directed, not so much to the survival of the fittest, as to the fitting of as many as possible to survive."[4] In the twentieth century the mistaken application of Darwin's theory served Hitler to subjugate other people in the name of racial fitness and colonize their territory in the name of obtaining adequate "living space." Social Darwinism is present today in the merciless struggle of competitors in the market-place, where the fit are the wealthy who ruthlessly exploit the poor and the powerless.

There is a mechanism in the economy that distributes the benefits of competition to everyone: this is the free market, governed by what Adam Smith called the "invisible hand." It acts equitably: if I do well for myself, I benefit not just myself but also my family, my company, and my community.

The market myth may be comforting for the rich, but it disregards the fact that the market distributes benefits only under conditions of near-perfect competition, where the playing field is level and the players have a more or less equal number of chips. In the real world, the playing field is not level and the distribution of wealth is strongly skewed. Under these conditions the market doesn't work equitably: the poorest 40 percent of the world is now left with 3 percent of the global wealth, while the wealth of the eight hundred billionaires of the world (though it plunged in 2009 to $2.4 trillion from $4.4 trillion the year before) equals the annual income of nearly half the world's peoples.

There is a strict equivalence between the size of your wallet and your personal worth as the owner of the wallet. The more you consume the better you are.

The equating of human worth with financial worth has been consciously fueled by business; companies advertised unlimited and even conspicuous consumption as the ideal. Fifty years ago retailing analyst Victor Lebow told us: "Our enormously productive economy demands that we make consumption our way of life, that we convert the buying and use of goods into rituals, that we seek our spiritual satisfaction, our ego satisfaction, in consumption. The economy needs things consumed, burned, worn out, replaced, and discarded at an ever-increasing rate."[5] The "consumption-equals-wealth-equals-happiness" myth fueled the world's consumption spree: in constant dollars, industrialized societies have consumed as many goods and services since 1950 as in all previous generations put together. Vast quantities of useful resources have been converted into toxic garbage, and the benefits have accrued mainly to self-concerned speculators who reap financial gains from every transaction, whether it serves a humanly and socially useful purpose or depletes precious resources and poisons the environment.

If other states possess natural resources we need for our economy, and if they hold beliefs and objectives that are different from and perhaps incompatible with ours—and if their leaders are not ready to accommodate our wishes—then we have the right to fight them: it's a "just war." In the final count, there are economic and political ends that justify military means.

In today's world, war is both a human and an ecological catastrophe. In addition to killing people, it damages productive lands, destroys habitations, and impairs vital balances in the local and the global ecology. Regardless what the problem is, war as its remedy is worse than its cause. Other than police action in immediate self-defense, warfare of any kind has become a crime against humanity and against all life on Earth.

VALUES AND CONSCIOUSNESS
IN THE ECOLOGICAL AGE

We now contrast this repertory of obsolete beliefs and dangerous myths with the kind of values and consciousness that would hallmark what Berry called the ecological age.[6]

The value of a person

In the ecological age the people held in highest esteem are not those who have amassed the greatest wealth and power for themselves but those who respect the balances and processes of nature and live in harmony with their fellows in society. The possession of money, and the material goods that money can buy, no longer serve as a measure of personal achievement. The symbol of social status is not a big house and powerful car, and the pinnacle of a life's accomplishment is not the yacht and the private jet. Being rich is defined by *being* and not by *having*. Real wealth is believed to lie in a fulfilling life, in the embrace of a loving family, healthy and happy children, a caring community, and a healthy environment. Living well doesn't exclude living comfortably, but comfort, and even luxury, are not measured by the quantity of the goods one owns but by the quality of his or her life experience.

The mission of education

Handing down the value of sustainability and harmony is basic to education. At all levels of education, from kindergarten to college, the mission of the school is not just to impart the skills and know-how that help students find lucrative employment, but to hand down the values on which a peaceful and sustainable society can be built and maintained. Schools are to enable young people to grow into locally active and globally thinking planetary citizens, living a healthy, productive, and responsible life.

The ecological age calls for a new consciousness, but a new

consciousness cannot be taught: it must emerge on its own. Ecological-age education is to foster the emergence of a new consciousness by contrasting the kind of world that results from following the dictates of the anthropocentric age, with the world that would emerge when a critical mass espouses values of sustainability, peace, and personal and social responsibility.

The nature of the new consciousness

The consciousness of the ecological age is new and at the same time age-old—it's a consciousness that's open to people and the world, in stark contrast to the ego-bound and brain-limited consciousness of the anthropocentric age. Thanks to the evolution of a "transpersonal" consciousness, people could come to feel their connections with the world in subtle and intuitive yet meaningful ways. They could sense that they are not separate entities pursuing independent destinies but interconnected elements of an integral reality.

Berry wrote that the primary aspect of the much-needed *Ecozoic period* in the checkered history of our species—a period that we could reach with concerted effort—"is that we recognize the larger community of life as our primary referent in terms of reality and value. This locating of the higher reality and the higher value in the larger community is absolutely primary. . . . All the human professions must recognize their prototype and their primary resource in the integral functioning of the earth community. The natural world itself is the primary economic reality, the primary educator, the primary governance, the primary healer, the primary presence of the sacred, the primary moral value."[7] The evolution of our consciousness would enable us to achieve this recognition, for it would be more than an abstract concept: it would be a directly felt, intimately experienced reality.

The experience of our connection with each other and the universe would inspire solidarity among people and empathy with all life on Earth. This would be the best, and possibly the only, way to recover the perennial intuition of oneness that is an essential part of our biological heritage.

IN SUMMARY

The shift from the anthropocentric age to the ecological age is first and foremost a shift in consciousness. It's in our own interest to foster and facilitate this shift at all levels in society, and in all areas of human endeavor.

In the first half of the twentieth century a consciousness-based worldshift was pure utopia. In the second half, it began to be discussed as a desirable alternative. And now, at the end of the first decade of the twenty-first century, it emerges not as an alternative but as the sole feasible way forward. There are no feasible alternatives to it.

If a shift in consciousness would remain mere utopia—a "no-place"—then it's to no-place to where our species would evolve: to extinction. But if a critical mass of forward-looking and responsible individuals would recognize that a consciousness-based worldshift is a real and realistic path to take, then humankind would evolve to a peaceful and sustainable *ecological age.*

Evolution or extinction is the choice before us. Berry had called attention to it almost before anyone else did. It's time to recognize the wisdom of his insight and set out on the path he had mapped for us.

Notes

CHAPTER 1. THE UNIVERSITY OF THE EARTH

1. Thomas Berry, *The Dream of the Earth* (San Francisco: Sierra Club Books, 1988), 91.
2. Ibid., 72.
3. Ibid., 197–98.

CHAPTER 3. SOME THOUGHTS ON THOMAS BERRY'S CONTRIBUTIONS TO THE WESTERN SPIRITUAL TRADITION

1. Teilhard de Chardin, *The Heart of Matter* (New York: Harcourt Brace Jovanovich, 1978), 26f.
2. Ibid., 71.
3. Teilhard de Chardin, *Hymn of the Universe* (New York: Harper & Row, 1961).
4. A letter written in 1920. See Robert Speaight, *The Life of Teilhard de Chardin* (New York: Harper & Row, 1967), 109.
5. Teilhard de Chardin, "Sketch of a Personalistic Universe," from *The Spirit of the Earth* (1931), v. 6 "Human Energy," translated by J. M. Cohen, 191.
6. Bruce Chilton, *Rabbi Paul: An Intellectual Biography* (New York: Doubleday, 2004), 249.
7. Thomas Berry, "The Earth: A New Context for Religious Unity," in Anne Lonergan and Caroline Richards, ed., *Thomas Berry and the New Cosmology* (Mystic, Conn.: Twenty-Third Publications, 1987), 38.

8. Berry, "The Earth."

9. Teilhard de Chardin, *The Heart of Matter*, 25.

10. Berry, *The Dream of the Earth* (San Francisco: Sierra Club Books, 1988), 211.

11. William Everson and Steven Herrmann, *The Shaman's Call: Interviews, Introduction, and Commentaries* (New York: Eloquent Books, 2009), 150.

12. Everson and Herrmann: *The Shaman's Call*, from Lee Bartlett's *The Sun Is But a Morning Star* (Albuquerque: University of New Mexicao Press, 1987).

13. Berry, *Dream of the Earth*, 207f.

14. Everson and Herrmann, *The Shaman's Call*, 162f.

15. Everson and Herrmann, *The Shaman's Call*, 155.

16. Thomas Berry, "Foreword," in Gabriele Uhlein, *Meditations with Hildegard of Bingen* (Santa Fe, N. Mex.: Bear & Co., 1983), 14.

17. Ibid.

18. See Matthew Fox, *Sheer Joy: Conversations with Thomas Aquinas on Creation Spirituality* (New York: Jeremy Tarcher/Putnam, 2003), 57.

19. See Matthew Fox, *Otto Rank as Mystic and Prophet in the Creation Spirituality Tradition*, in www.matthewfox.org, "recent articles."

20. Fox, *Sheer Joy*, 97.

21. Ibid.

22. Berry, *The Dream of the Earth*, 215.

23. Fox, *Sheer Joy*, 97.

24. Ibid., 89.

25. Ibid., 95.

26. Ibid., 87.

CHAPTER 4. THOMAS BERRY AND
THE EVOCATION OF PARTICIPATORY CONSCIOUSNESS

1. Thomas Berry, *The Dream of the Earth* (San Francisco: Sierra Club Books, 1988), x.

2. Thomas Berry, *Evening Thoughts: Reflecting on Earth as Sacred Community* (San Francisco: Sierra Club Books, 2006), 10.

3. Thomas Berry, *Evening Thoughts: Reflecting on Earth as Sacred Community* (San Francisco: Sierra Club Books, 2006), 51.

4. Berry, *Evening Thoughts*, 137.

5. Berry, *Dream of the Earth*, 215.

6. Ibid., 198.

7. Ibid., 223.

8. Berry, *Great Work,* 12–13, 20.

9. Berry, *Evening Thoughts,* 83.

10. Ibid., 64.

11. Ibid., 40.

12. Ibid., 21.

13. Berry, *The Dream of the Earth,* 205.

14. Berry, *Evening Thoughts,* 59–60.

15. Ibid., 69.

16. Ibid., 55.

17. Berry, *The Dream of the Earth,* 197.

18. Ibid., 198.

19. Berry, *Evening Thoughts,* 130.

20. Berry, *The Dream of the Earth,* 211–12.

21. Berry, *Evening Thoughts,* 137.

22. Berry, *The Great Work,* 17.

23. Berry, *Evening Thoughts,* 18.

CHAPTER 5. INSCENDENCE: THE KEY
TO THE GREAT WORK OF OUR TIME

1. Thomas Berry, *The Dream of the Earth* (San Francisco: Sierra Club Books, 1988), 207–8.

2. Ibid., 211.

3. Ibid., 201.

4. Ibid., 211.

5. Thomas Berry, *The Great Work: Our Way into the Future* (New York: Bell Tower, 1999), 57.

6. Ibid., 174–75.

7. Thomas Berry, *Evening Thoughts: Reflecting on Earth as Sacred Community* (San Francisco: Sierra Club Books, 2006), 26.

8. Ibid., 173–74.

9. Berry, *The Dream of the Earth,* 209.

10. Ibid., 208.

11. Berry, *Evening Thoughts,* 25.

12. All quotes in this sentence are from *Evening Thoughts,* 25–27.

13. Ibid., 25.

14. Rainer Maria Rilke, *Rilke's Book of Hours: Love Poems to God,* trans. Anita Barrows and Joanna Macy (New York: Riverhead Books, 1996), 95.

15. Ibid., 116.

16. Ibid.

17. Bill Plotkin, *Soulcraft: Crossing into the Mysteries of Nature and Psyche* (Novato, Calif.: New World Library, 2003), 11–12.

18. Berry, *The Great Work,* 159.

19. Berry, *The Dream of the Earth,* 211–12.

20. Berry, *The Great Work,* 163.

21. Ibid., 55.

22. Ibid., 159.

23. Ibid., 165.

24. Ibid., 201.

25. Ibid., 53.

26. Berry, *The Dream of the Earth,* 194.

27. Ibid., 208.

28. Berry, *The Great Work,* 160.

29. Ibid., 171–72.

30. Ibid., 172.

31. Berry, *Evening Thoughts*, 23.

32. Ibid., 17.

33. Berry, *The Great Work,* 165.

34. Berry, *The Dream of the Earth,* 165.

35. Berry, *The Great Work,* 165.

36. Berry, *Evening Thoughts,* 145.

37. Berry, *The Great Work,* 79.

38. Ibid., 165.

39. Berry, *The Dream of the Earth,* 195.

40. Ibid.

41. Berry, *The Great Work,* 115.

42. Ibid., 55.

43. Berry, *Evening Thoughts,* 145. The universe's guidance is also described in Brian Swimme and Thomas Berry, *The Universe Story: From the Primordial Flaring Forth to the Ecozoic Era—a Celebration of the Unfolding of the Cosmos* (New York: HarperCollins, 1992) and in Brian Swimme, *The Hidden Heart of the Cosmos* (Maryknoll, N.Y.: Orbis Books, 1996).

44. Berry, *The Dream of the Earth,* 196.

45. Ibid., 197.

46. Ibid., 197–98.

47. Ibid., 201.

48. Ibid., 195.

49. Bill Plotkin, *Nature and the Human Soul: Cultivating Wholeness and Community in a Fragmented World* (Novato, Calif.: New World Library, 2008), 40.

50. See Joanna Macy, *Mutual Causality in Buddhism and General Systems Theory: The Dharma of Natural Systems* (Albany, N.Y.: State University of New York Press, 1991).

51. Personal communication, March 16, 2006.

52. Berry, *Evening Thoughts,* 145.

53. Berry, *The Great Work,* 201.

CHAPTER 6. DREAMING IN SACRED SITES

1. Thomas Berry, *Evening Thoughts: Reflecting on Earth as Sacred Community* (San Francisco: Sierra Club Books, 2006).

2. Thomas Berry and Brian Swimme, *The Universe Story* (San Francisco: Harper, 1992).

3. Thomas Berry, *The Dream of the Earth* (San Francisco: Sierra Club Books, 1988)

4. Thomas Berry, *Befriending the Earth* (Mystic, Conn.: Twenty-Third Publications, 1991).

5. Rhea White, "Dissociation, narrative, and exceptional human experiences." In S. Krippner and S. M. Powers, *Broken Images, Broken Selves: Dissociative Narratives in Clinical Practice* (Washington, D.C.: Brunner/Mazel, 1997), 88–121.

6. Thomas Berry, *The Great Work: Our Way into the Future* (New York: Bell Tower, 1999).

7. Paul Devereux, "The Archaeology of Consciousness," *Journal for Scientific Exploration* 4 (1997): 527–38.

8. V. Deloria Jr., "Reflection and Revelation: Knowing Land, Places and Ourselves." In J. A. Swan, ed., *The Power of Place and Human Environments* (Wheaton, Ill.: Theosophical Publishing House, 2000), 28–40.

9. R. Otto, *The Idea of the Holy* (Oxford: Oxford University Press, 1924), 30.

10. J. Swan, (1988). "Sacred places in nature and transpersonal experience," *ReVision* 10 (1988): 21–26.

11. V. Deloria Jr., *Reflection and Revelation,* 35.

12. D. E. Walker, "Durkheim, Eliade, and Sacred Geography in Northwestern North America," *University of Oregon Anthropological Papers* 52 (1996): (Eugene, Ore.: University of Oregon), 63–68.

13. C. Crumley, "Sacred Landscapes: Constructed and Conceptualized." In W. Ashmore and A. Knapp, eds., *Archaeologies of Landscape* (Oxford: Blackwell, 1999): 269–76.

14. Paul Devereux, *The Sacred Place* (London: Cassell, 2000), 24.

15. D. Eck, "India's Tirthas: Crossings in Sacred Geography," *History of Religions* 20 (1981): 323–44.

16. Stanley Krippner and A. Thompson, "A 10-facet Model of dreaming applied to dream practices of sixteen Native American cultural groups," *Dreaming* 6 (1996): 71–96.

17. Paul Devereux, "The Archaeology of Consciousness," 4, 527–38.

18. C. Crumley, "Sacred Landscapes: Constructed and Conceptualized," 269–76.

19. D. E. Walker, "Durkheim, Eliade, and sacred geography in Northwestern North America," 63–68.

20. J. R. Hale, J. Z. de Boer, J. P. Chanton, and H. A. Spiller, "Questioning the Delphic Oracle," *Scientific American* (July 13, 2003): 1–5.

21. D. Carmichael, "Places of power: Mescalero Apache sacred sites and sensitive areas." In D. Carmichael, J. Hubert, B. Reeves, and A. Schanche, eds., *Sacred Sites, Sacred Places* (London: Routledge, 1994), 90–98.

22. Lawrence Durrell, *The Listener,* September 25, 1947.

23. J. Antrobus, "Characteristics of dreams." In M. A. Carskadon, ed., *Encyclopedia of Sleep and Dreaming* (New York: Macmillan, 1993), 98–101.

24. The technical details of this study, along with a careful analysis of the results, are reported in the Devereux et al. study cited above.

25. Joseph Campbell, *The Mythic Image* (Princeton, N.J.: Princeton University Press, 1974), 190.

26. D. E. Walker, "Durkheim, Eliade, and Sacred Geography in Northwestern North America," 63–68.

27. Paul Devereux, J. Steele, and D. Kubrin *Earthmind* (New York: Harper & Row, 1989).

28. Paul Devereux, *Places of Power: Measuring the Secret Energy of Ancient Sites,* 2nd ed. (London: Cassell, 1999), 155.

29. P. F. Sheeran, "Place and power," *ReVision* 13 (1990): 28–32.

30. R. G. Jahn, P. Devereux, and M. Ibison, "Acoustical Resonances of Assorted Ancient Structures," *Journal of the Acoustical Society of America* 99, no. 2 (1996): 649–58.

31. Paul Devereux, *Secrets of Ancient and Sacred Places: The World's Mysterious Heritage* (London: Blandford, 1992); Paul Devereux, *Places of Power,* 154–55, 175–83.

32. R. G. Jahn, P. Devereux, and M. Ibison "Acoustical Resonances."

33. I. A. Cook, "Ancient Acoustic Resonance Patterns Influence Regional Brain Activity," *ICRL Internal Technical Report,* Princeton: International Consciousness Research Laboratories (2003).

34. Thomas Berry, *The Dream of the Earth; Befriending the Earth;* and *The Great Work.*

35. D. Lee, ed. and trans, *Plato: Timaeas and Critia* (Harmondsworth, U.K.: Penguin, 1965).

36. D. Feinstein, "At Play in the Fields of the Mind: Personal Myths as Fields of Information," *Journal of Humanistic Psychology* 38 (2000): 71–109.

37. Devereux, P. *Places of Power.*

38. S. Larsen, S. "Ecology and the Archaic Psyche," *Psyche: The Ecopsychology Newsletter* (Spring 1995): 3.

39. E. J. Roberts, "Place and the Human Spirit," *The Humanistic Psychologist* 26 (1998): 5–34.

40. E. J. Roberts, "Place and the Human Spirit," 530.

41. Acknowledgments: The authors would like to thank Robert L. Van de Castle for his helpful suggestions, Andrew Delpino and Steve Hart for clerical and editorial support, Marena Koukis for serving as judge, and Robert Tartz for his statistical analysis of the data. They are also grateful to Gabrielle Hawkes, who transcribed the bulk of the audio-recorded dream reports as well as facilitating many of the on-site sessions. Finally, thanks are due to the volunteer dreamers and their helpers, without whom there would be no "sacred site" dream data to analyze. This study was supported by Saybrook University's Chair for the Study of Consciousness and by the Dragon Project Trust.

CHAPTER 7. THE DOUBLE LIFE OF THOMAS BERRY

1. Duane Elgin, *The Living Universe* (San Francisco: Berrett-Koehler, 2009).
2. David Bohm, *Wholeness and the Implicate Order* (London: Routledge & Kegan Paul, 1980), 11.
3. David Bohm, *Wholeness and the Implicate Order,* 191.
4. Brian Swimme, *The Hidden Heart of the Cosmos* (New York: Orbis Books, 1996), 100.
5. See the discussion in my book, *Promise Ahead* (New York: Quill Books, 2000), 52–57.
6. Thomas Berry, "The Spirituality of the Earth," in Charles Birch, et. al. (eds.) *Liberating Life: Contemporary Approaches in Ecological Theology* (Eugene Origon: Wipf & Stock, 1990).
7. Thomas Berry, *The Dream of the Earth*, 48–49.
8. Ibid.
9. Thomas Berry, "The Spirituality of the Earth."

CHAPTER 8. ECOLOGICAL INTERIORITY

1. Thomas Berry, *The Dream of the Earth* (San Francisco: Sierra Club Books, 1988).
2. Brian Swimme and Thomas Berry, *The Universe Story: From the Primordial Flaring Forth to the Ecozoic Era; A Celebration of the Unfolding of the Cosmos* (San Francisco: HarperCollins, 1992).
3. Thomas Berry, *The Great Work: Our Way into the Future* (New York: Bell Tower, 1999).
4. Ken Wilber, *Sex, Ecology, Spirituality: The Spirit of Evolution* (Boston: Shambhala, 1995); *A Brief History of Everything* (Boston: Shambhala, 1996); and *The Eye of Spirit: An Integral Vision for a World Gone Slightly Mad* (Boston: Shambhala, 1997).
5. Drew Dellinger, personal communication, July 11, 2003.
6. Sean Esbjörn-Hargens, ed. *Integral Ecology*. Special Double Issue of *World Futures: The Journal of General Evolution* 61 (2005), nos. 1–2.
7. The title of this paper was "Integral Ecology: A Post-metaphysical approach to Environmental Phenomena." Later I also published a summative article with the same title in *AQAL: The Journal of Integral Theory and Practice.*
8. Sean Esbjörn-Hargens and Michael E. Zimmerman, *Integral Ecology: Uniting*

Multiple Perspectives on the Natural World (Boston: Integral Books, 2009).

9. H. B. Moore, *Marine Ecology* (New York: John Wiley & Sons, Inc. 1958), 7.

10. Ibid.

11. L. Boff and V. Elizondo, eds., *Ecology and Poverty: Cry of the Earth, Cry of the Poor* (London: SCM Press, 1995), ix–x.

12. Ken Wilber, *Sex, Ecology, Spirituality.*

13. Sean Esbjörn-Hargens and Michael E. Zimmerman, *Integral Ecology*, 8.

14. Ibid., 168–69.

15. The earliest version of this quote I'm aware of is found in *The Universe Story* and reads, "That the universe is a communion of subjects rather than a collection of objects is the central commitment of the Ecozoic. Existence itself is derived from and sustained by this intimacy of each being with every other being of the universe" (Swimme & Berry, 1992, p. 243). Another version of this quote then appeared almost a decade later as one of the ten basic rights of Berry's (2001) articulation of Earth jurisprudence. Number three reads in full: "The universe is composed of subjects to be communed with, not of objects to be exploited. As subjects, each component of the universe is capable of having rights." A year later Berry (2002) published a shorter version of these ten rights in the magazine *Resurgence* under the title "Rights of the Earth: Earth Democracy." Then most recently Berry (2006) published a revised version of these precepts in appendix 2 as one of the Ten Principles for Jurisprudence Revision. Here number three reads: "The universe is composed of subjects to be communed with, not primarily of objects to be used. As a subject, each component of the universe is capable of having rights" (p. 149). As these four versions indicate, this quote was a basic tenet in Berry's "integral vision" and showed up in slight variations throughout his talks and writings. Note: Angyal (2003) appears to misquote Berry with respect to number three, as his number three doesn't match the source he cites (Berry, 2001).

16. M. Bekoff, "Foreword," in Esbjörn-Hargens and Zimmerman, *Integral Ecology*, xx.

17. Ibid.

18. Thomas Berry, *The Dream of the Earth,* 133.

19. Thomas Berry, "The Spirituality of the Earth," in Charles Birch, et. al. (eds.) *Liberating Life: Contemporary Approaches in Ecological Theology* (Eugene. Ore.: Wipf & Stock, 1990), 15X.

20. Ibid.

21. M. E. Tucker, "Appendix 3: Editor's Afterword: An Intellectual Biography of Thomas Berry." In Thomas Berry, *Evening Thoughts: Reflecting on Earth as Sacred Community* (San Francisco: Sierra Club Books, 2006), 163.

22. Thomas Berry, "The Spirituality of the Earth," 15X.

23. Thomas Berry, "Teilhard in the Ecological Age," in *Teilhard in the 21st Century: The Emerging Spirit of Earth*. A. Fabel, and D. St. John, eds. (Maryknoll, N.Y.: Orbis Books, 2003).

24. Thomas Berry, "The Spirituality of the Earth, 15X.

25. Pierre Teilhard de Chardin, *The Phenomena of Man* (St. James Place, London: Collins Sons & Co Ltd., 1959), 56.

26. Ibid., 57.

27. Thomas Berry, "The Spirituality of the Earth," 15X.

28. Thomas Berry, *The Sacred Universe: Earth, Spirituality, and Religion in the Twenty-first Century* (New York: Columbia University Press, 2009), 1.

29. Thomas Berry, *Evening Thoughts*.

30. M. Bekoff, *Minding Animals: Awareness, Emotions, and Heart* (New York: Oxford University Press, 2002); *Animal Passions and Beastly Virtues: Reflections on Redecorating Nature* (Philadelphia: Temple University Press, 2006); and *The Emotional Lives of Animals: A Leading Scientist Explores Animal Joy, Sorrow, and Empathy—and Why They Matter* (Novato, Calif.: New World Library, 2007).

31. Joel Berger, *The Better to Eat You With: Fear in the Animal World* (Chicago: Chicago University Press, 2008).

32. G. A. Bradshaw, *Elephants on the Edge: What Animals Teach Us about Humanity* (New Haven, Conn.: Yale University Press, 2009).

33. I encourage everyone to check out Dellinger's collection of poems, *Love Letter to the Milky Way* (www.drewdellinger.org).

CHAPTER 10. BERRY AND THE SHIFT FROM THE ANTHROPOCENTRIC TO THE ETHOLOGICAL AGE

1. Thomas Berry, "The Ecological Age," in *The Dream of the Earth* (San Francisco: Sierra Club Books, 1988), 42.

2. Thomas Berry, "The Dream of the Earth: Our Way Into the Future," in *The Dream of the Earth* (San Francisco: Sierra Club Books, 1988), 202.

3. Based on Ervin Laszlo, *Quantum Shift in the Global Brain* (Rochester, Vt.: Inner Traditions, 2008), and *WorldShift 2012* (Rochester, Vt.: Inner Traditions, 2009). By permission of the publisher.

4. Thomas H. Huxley, ed. "The Struggle for Existence in Human Society," in *Evolution and Ethics and Other Essays* (New York and London: Appleton, 1925).

5. Quoted by Alan Durning in *How Much Is Enough?* (New York: Norton, 1992), 22.

6. A more detailed account is given in Ervin Laszlo, *WorldShift 2012.*

7. Thomas Berry, *The Emerging Ecozoic Period,* this volume, pp. 9–15.

Contributors

Allan Combs is professor of Transformative Studies at the California Institute of Integral Studies (CIIS) in San Francisco and the author and coauthor of more than 100 publications on consciousness and ecology, including *Synchronicity* and *The Radiance of Being,* the best-book award-winner of the Scientific and Medical Network, and recently *Consciousness Explained Better: An Integral Understanding of Consciousness.*

Paul Devereux is an independent scholar and lecturer, focusing largely on anthropologies of consciousness, cognitive aspects of archaeology, and archaeoacoustics—the study of sound at ancient sacred sites. He is founding editor of *Time & Mind* and has written 27 books as well as many articles for general publication. His latest book is *Sacred Geography.*

Sean Esbjörn-Hargens is an associate professor and founding chair of the department of Integral Theory at JFK University in Pleasant Hill, California. He is director of both the Integral Research Center and the Integral Ecology Center and executive editor of the *Journal of Integral Theory and Practice.* Sean is coauthor of *Integral Ecology: Uniting Multiple Perspectives on the Natural World* and the editor of *Integral Theory in Action* (SUNY, 2010).

Duane Elgin is an internationally recognized visionary speaker, author, and educator. His books include *The Living Universe, Promise Ahead, Voluntary Simplicity,* and *Awakening Earth.* He has worked as a senior staff member of the Presidential Commission on the American Future and as a senior social scientist with the think tank SRI International, where he coauthored numerous studies of the future.

Adam Fish, M.A., Cinema and Media Studies, UCLA, is a graduate student in UCLA's department of anthropology.

Matthew Fox "might well be the most creative, the most comprehensive, surely the most challenging religious-spiritual teacher in America" (in the words of Thomas Berry). Fox is the author of *Original Blessing; The Reinvention of Work; Creativity: Where the Divine and the Human Meet; One River, Many Wells: Wisdom Springing from Global Faiths,* and numerous other books. He was a member of the Dominican Order for thirty-four years.

Geneen Marie Haugen is a writer, wilderness wanderer, and guide to the intertwined mysteries of nature and psyche. Her creative nonfiction and eco-essays have appeared in many anthologies and journals, including *American Nature Writing* and the syndicated column "Writers on the Range." She is a former tipi dweller and whitewater river guide who now lives in the slickrock lands of southern Utah.

Stanley Krippner is professor of psychology at Saybrook University, San Francisco. He is a recipient of the American Psychological Association's Award for Distinguished Contributions to the International Advancement. He is coauthor of *Extraordinary Dreams, Personal Mythology, Haunted by Combat: Understanding PTSD in War Veterans,* and co-editor of *Varieties of Anomalous Experience* and *Mysterious Minds: The Neurobiology of Psychics, Mediums, and Other Remarkable People.*

Ervin Laszlo is a pioneer in systems philosophy and general systems theory and founder of the field of general evolution theory. A rare combination of scholar, theorist, and activist, Laszlo is former Director of Research for the United Nations and advisor to the director-general of UNESCO. He is also the author of a major Club of Rome study on goals for humanity and the founder and president of the Club of Budapest, dedicated to focusing the combined vision of the humanities, arts, and spirituality, as well as science, on global betterment. He is the author of more than 100 books and articles dedicated to sustainability and the future of humanity.

Joanna Macy is a teacher, author, and the creator of *The Work That Reconnects*. Drawing from Buddhist practices, systems theory, and a love of life, her workshops empower environmental and social activists worldwide. Her many books include *Coming Back to Life: Practices to Reconnect Our Lives, Our World; World As Lover, World As Self; Widening Circles, A Memoir*; and translations of Rilke's poetry. For information about Joanna Macy and her work see www.joannamacy.net.

Bill Plotkin is a depth psychologist and wilderness guide. As founder of western Colorado's Animas Valley Institute in 1981, he has guided thousands of women and men through nature-based initiatory passages. He is the author of *Soulcraft: Crossing into the Mysteries of Nature and Psyche* and *Nature and the Human Soul: Cultivating Wholeness and Community in a Fragmented World.*

Robert Tartz is an independent researcher who has published a variety of articles in peer-reviewed journals in quantitative dream content analysis with an emphasis in cross-cultural and gender differences. He is listed in *Who's Who in America, Who's Who in Science and Engineering,* and *Who's Who in Finance and Business.*

David Woolfson is an attorney and global activist based in Canada. As an activist, he focuses on the many challenges and opportunities that face humanity today. He is dedicated to promoting new thinking and actions to address the major social and environmental challenges of our time. He has initiated and been a major participant in numerous organizations and initiatives including the World Wisdom Alliance, the Club of Budapest (Canada), and the World Wisdom Council.

Index